INSTANT DREAM HOME

A Paint-by-Numbers Interior Design Guide

DARCY KEMPTON

Photography by Diana Thai

All Interior Designed & Created by the Talented & Dedicated Team of Simply Stunning Spaces™

WWW.SIMPLYSTUNNINGSPACES.NET

For everyone who desires to live in a home that looks and feels like the place they just can't wait to come home to.

6	INTRODUCTION
10	ABOUT THE AUTHOR
17	MEET OUR CLIENTS
99	STEP 1: INSPIRATION
133	STEP 2: DESIGN PLANNING
181	STEP 3: TAKE ACTION
191	CASE STUDY
219	IMAGINE THE POSSIBILITIES
255	THE BUSINESS OF DESIGN
260	STAY IN TOUCH
262	ACKNOWLEDGEMENTS

WELCOME

INTRODUCTION

Let's face the facts.

FACT NUMBER ONE: THE QUALITY OF OUR LIFE IS DIRECTLY DICTATED BY THE QUALITY OF OUR SURROUNDINGS.
Think about this for just a moment. Imagine yourself working from an office where the walls are white, the furniture is drab and uncomfortable, the carpet is dingy and the lighting is poor. How does that make you feel?

Now, imagine what it would be like if you were working in an office with large picture windows, stylish comfortable chairs, blue walls adorned with tranquil photos of the ocean, and an organizational system that keeps everything in its place. How does that make you feel? Where do you think you would be happier working?

That question is rhetorical if you ask me, because who wouldn't prefer a beautiful space over an unattractive one if given the option?

The same thing goes with reference to our homes. How do you think it would make you feel to come home to a space that was beautiful, inviting, organized and harmonious? The only difference between our homes and our offices is that we hold the power to deciding how our homes look and feel, not anyone else. So why is it then, that our homes are not evoking the feelings of peace, harmony and beauty we're longing for?

When we first move into a new home, the feelings of excitement and newness propel most of us towards trying to make this new space everything we imagined it to be when we first saw it. We're inspired and eager to decorate it because we want to make our new house feel like a home.

With this excitement soon comes the feeling of complete overwhelm, and then sadly, after weeks of searching, buying, trying and returning items for your home, frustration and defeat set in. Life gets busy and your family, work, spouse and friends quickly take priority, leaving you with a home that feels 'good enough for now'.

Before you know it years go by, and you realize you're still living in 'good enough for now' but now 'good enough' doesn't seem to look so good at all. A renewed desire to finish your home has been sparked; perhaps it was by a home remodeling show on HGTV, a magazine you picked up, or a friend's house that you've been envying.

Reflecting back on your experience of decorating your home, you might start to remember those feelings of frustration and exhaustion are already starting to bubble. This time, before you buy a single item, you start asking for help. You'll probably ask your friend who's home you envied how she did it; get her opinion and then a few others, trying to piece together everyone's advice. The problem is, they all have different opinions that leave you even more uncertain. Perhaps it was then that you started looking online for some professional advice.

So what did you discover?

FACT NUMBER TWO: HIRING AN INTERIOR DESIGNER IS EXPENSIVE.

If money were no obstacle, then having a home you loved would be simple. You would just call up an Interior Designer, write your big fat check and presto-change-o, you would have a beautiful home in no time, right? Nice for those people, but what about everyone else?

The truth is, most established interior designers won't take on small projects with small budgets. They are accustomed to making their profit from the sale of goods that go into your home. If you don't have a lot of remodeling or furnishing to do, then there's no incentive for a designer to want to work for you.

So then, where does that leave you?

FACT NUMBER THREE: YOU'RE DREAM HOME IS JUST AROUND THE CORNER.

I have spent over ten years designing homes, offices, restaurants, bars, boutique hotels and everything in between. I've worked with celebrities, Fortune 500 Corporations, and I've worked with hundreds of homeowners just like you. I have built my interior design business based on the same simple formula that I'm revealing to you in the pages of this book, Instant Dream Home.

My goal with *Instant Dream Home* is to help open your mind to the realm of possibilities that are well within your reach; as well as provide you with a simple solution you can use to have a home you love. Quickly, easily and affordably.

This book illustrates my three-step process to interior decorating success.

Step one is about helping you define your style through inspiration. This is usually the easiest and most fun part of the design process but also a very important one to gaining clarity in regards to the new home you're about to create.

WELCOME

Step two focuses on your design plan. I will take you through my process of creating a plan that will be functional, affordable, stylish and perfect for your lifestyle. My goal is to give you some sound ground for making any big remodeling decisions and help you choose décor that will fit your home.

Step three provides you with the tools and information you need to take action. This section covers everything you need to know in order to start implementing a design plan that is brilliantly well planned, practical and stylish.

Within these 263 pages I will also share stories with you from past clients of mine. To help get your creative vibes flowing I have included some of my favorite projects such as: Pooch Hotels by Petco, Bruce Buffer, Host of the UFC, Kiptyn Locke from ABC's, "The Bachelorette" and Business Moguls Lisa Sasevich and Mike Koenigs.

You will also find some wonderful bonus gifts along the way and some fun, entertaining videos to keep you engaged. You'll also see case studies from homeowners just like you who have followed this book's principals and have stunning results to show for it.

This likely may not be the first book on decorating you purchase, but my hope is that it's the last one you will ever need. By following the steps I have laid out in Instant Dream Home, I'm certain you will be closer to your dream home than you ever imagined.

Happy Reading and Happy Decorating!

Sincerely,

Darcy K.

ABOUT THE AUTHOR

DARCY K.

Growing up in the small town of Colchester, Vermont, I wasn't exposed to very much in the way of interior design. However, I can say that my parents always had at least one D.I.Y. remodeling project underway at all times. I always had my hands on something creative and spent most of my free time either painting, drawing or sewing.

My parents taught me at an early age that in order to get what I wanted, I had to work hard. At twelve years old that meant a paper route, babysitting, and making hair scrunchies to sell to the girls at school. This work ethic carried me through to college.

During high school I had an art teacher I'll never forget. I remember telling her I wanted to go to college for biology, but she strongly encouraged me to do something more creative. This encouragement led me towards a degree at Virginia Tech in Interior Design, laying the foundation for my future career. I knew I was going to have my own interior design company someday but first I spent several years

ABOUT THE AUTHOR

working for other interior design firms. I was continuously astounded when I saw what people would spend on the interior design of their home. It was absurd I thought, "Don't they know they can get something similar for much less?"

I knew what I wanted to do when I started my own company and that was to find a way to bring interior design services down to the everyday homeowner.

Although I can't deny that large design budgets are fun to work with, I personally enjoy the challenge of creating designer-looks-for-less and coaching people through the process of transforming their houses, into homes.

Through the process of building my business I made it a constant habit to surround myself with inspiring entrepreneurs I respect, like: Lisa Sasevich, Mike Koenigs, Michael Eisner, Robert Allen, John Assaraf and many others. I gained branding strategies from some of the World's leading female designers like Donna Karan and Kathy Ireland. I've also had the

HGTV's Belma Johnson

SIMPLY STUNNING

Kiptyn Locke,
ABC's The Bachelorette

Summer Baltzer,
HGTV's Design on a Dime

ABOUT THE AUTHOR

honor of working alongside HGTV's "Designed to Sell", Belma Michael Johnson and have been featured on San Diego's Channel 6 News, San Diego Magazine and Texas Home & Living. I've also had the opportunity to meet public figures Hilary Clinton and Arnold Schwarzenegger.

With well over a decade of experience putting my skills to the test, I've made just about every decorating mistake in the book.

As a result, I have some really great shortcuts to share with you to help you avoid these same mistakes.

I believe everyone deserves to have a home they love and more importantly, it shouldn't have to cost a fortune. Instant Dream Home will provide you with a roadmap that you can use to take the properly calculated steps towards creating your dream home. No matter how long it takes you to achieve it, enjoy the journey. Decorating and remodeling should be fun so go ahead, turn the pages and start learning how to love your home and love your life!

Donna Karan, DKNY

Kathy Ireland

SIMPLY STUNNING

Hilary Clinton

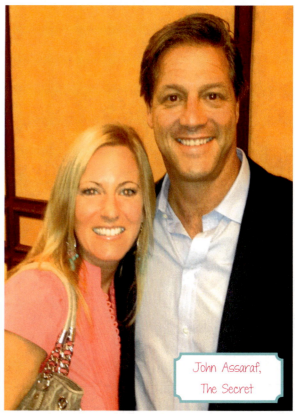
John Assaraf, The Secret

Lisa Sasevich, Queen of Sales Conversion

Arnold Schwarzenegger

MEET OUR CLIENTS

> " Darcy, as this year comes to an end I just wanted to thank you again for all you did with my house. You're incredible at what you do and the time and energy you put into my house on such a small budget was amazing. Thank you so much!!!
> -Kiptyn Locke, ABC's "The Bachelorette" Season 5 "

KIPTYN LOCKE

As Seen On: abc The BACHELORETTE

MEET OUR CLIENTS

BACHELOR PAD IN PARADISE

KIPTYN LOCKE'S MODERN SURFER'S PARADISE IS REVEALED ON CAMERA

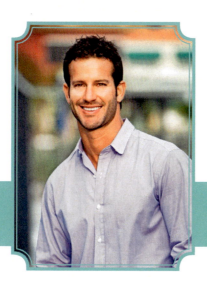

BIO: Kiptyn appeared as a hopeful bachelor on Season 5 of ABC's "The Bachelorette" and has since then raised over $5 million supporting various charities over the past five years.

MEET OUR CLIENTS

BACHELOR PAD IN PARADISE

KIPTYN LOCKE'S MODERN SURFER'S PARADISE IS REVEALED ON CAMERA

I live for the "WOW!" moments that I get from my clients when they see their newly designed home for the first time. My goal is to give every client that jaw-dropping Design Show moment, which is easy to do with clients as busy as mine. Kiptyn was certainly one of those clients, and when I heard that he was going to be leaving for Hawaii for a week I jumped on the opportunity to make one of those moments happen. I asked my friend Belma Johnson (former Host of HGTV's "Designed to Sell") to help me with the production and we were able to get the whole event on camera.

Kiptyn, who was formerly on ABC's Hit Reality Show "The Bachelorette," was familiar with being on camera and was happy to participate. My team and I had one week to transform Kiptyn's old home into a modern bachelor pad, and with most of that week spent in the preparation process of gathering materials and furnishings, we only had one day to pull everything together. My team and I documented our steps in real-time action to show you our tips and tricks on designing a perfect home. To see my team and I in action…

BACHELOR PAD IN PARADISE

Female Eye for the Single Guy

Check out Kiptyn's "Jaw-dropping Reaction"
at: www.female-eye.com

MEET OUR CLIENTS

Kiptyn had come to me in need of a bachelor pad makeover. At the time, he was living in a home with very little personal touch and sleeping on a mattress on the floor. I made it my goal to help Kiptyn get excited about this new chapter in his life with a warm and welcoming place to come home to every night.

Kiptyn's house had great potential from the get go, and it was my job to help it come alive. Nestled in the middle of one of my favorite little beach towns in San Diego and walking distance from the ocean, Kiptyn's home had everything from wood floors to an amazing layout. However, if you were to walk through the living room you would notice there wasn't a single piece of artwork or photography to be seen. The walls were barren, and the décor lacking. Kiptyn was in need of a woman's touch, and this is what sparked our pilot: "Female Eye for the Single Guy." To see this pilot, along with some of my other decorating videos, visit simplystunningspaces.net/videos.

The first step in transforming Kiptyn's home was deciding on a color scheme. My inspiration was his rug. In a home lacking of much personal touch, it was clear that this rug was something that Kiptyn was happy with. My team and I used the rugs color and pattern as a model for the rest of his house.

Before

BACHELOR PAD IN PARADISE

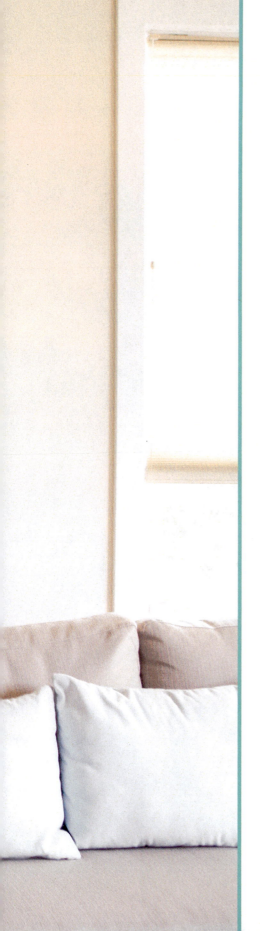

Getting back to the color scheme, you can see from the video that all of the colors that we used in the living room were pulled from the rug. The pillows we used on the sofa, the artwork we chose for the walls, and the accessories we used in candles and centerpieces were all pulled back into the colors from the rug. One of the simplest decorating tips to making your house feel more personal is adding framed pictures and artwork to your walls.

BACHELOR PAD IN PARADISE

Kiptyn loves to entertain. So, we made sure to add a mini bar to his living area and give an update to his fire pit. Adding a modern touch to your home can be as simple as replacing the Duraflame log from your fire pit with some broken glass, which can be bought from American Fire Glass.

MEET OUR CLIENTS

The next step was to get his mattress off the floor and give Kiptyn a "big boy bed." With a modern bed frame, a new comforter and some pillows, the room was already undergoing a big improvement. In addition, we moved the electronics into the closet to hide the spider web of cords and cleaned Kiptyn's nightstands up by giving him hanging pendants. As you can see, you don't need to spend a fortune to make a big difference in your home. With just a few adjustments we were able to completely transform Kiptyn's bedroom.

The key to personalizing your home is paying attention to the details. Little accessories, such as pillows or artwork, can make a huge statement. In Kiptyn's bedroom I used one of my favorite tricks: replacing nightstand lamps with hanging pendants, which adds dimension and saves precious nightstand space.

Before

After

Before

SIMPLYSTUNNINGSPACES.NET 29

Beyond just the looks of your home, you must also put thought into functionality. Never skimp on the comfort of your home. For example, your sheets. When decorating a home, many people will purchase lower quality linens to save a few dollars, but this will be regretted very quickly. Your sheets are something that you are going to be enjoying (or hating) every single night, so spending the extra few dollars for a high

thread count is a good idea. On the same thought, window treatments can be an important part of any bedroom. If you are a light sleeper, or frequently find yourself waking up earlier than you would like to sun seeping through your curtains, black out shades are a good investment.

MEET OUR CLIENTS

Another key aspect in the functionality of your home is insuring that workspace and living space remain divided. To avoid Kiptyn being tempted to take his computer into his bedroom or living room to work we made him a designated office space downstairs. Having a designated workspace will keep you organized and help you get your work done with fewer distractions.

To make Kiptyn's office accommodating I used another one of my favorite tricks. Using whiteboard paint my team and I made a border around his office, which he could then use to make notes on. Whiteboard paint is a great tool that can be used for many different purposes. However, you should be careful to avoid painting an entire wall with it, as the white color would be bland and boring. In my video you can see the whiteboard paint at use in Kiptyn's office, and how we used it as a border with a bold color above and below it to keep the room interesting.

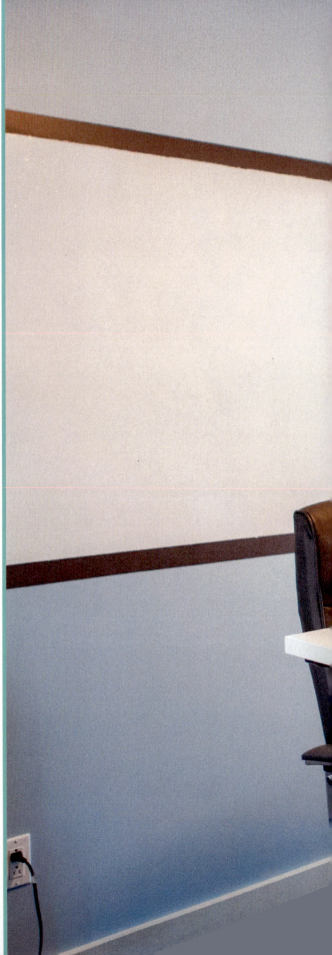

> I love using whiteboard paint in offices. It's always a hit.

MEET OUR CLIENTS

BACHELOR PAD IN PARADISE

In the end, Kiptyn was ecstatic to have his new home ready for entertaining. With the modern color scheme and style, Kiptyn's home reflected his personality. The functionality of his new home would allow him to both work and entertain. Kiptyn's home went under a huge transformation, and all under a budget of $10,000, proving that decorating your home doesn't have to cost you a fortune.

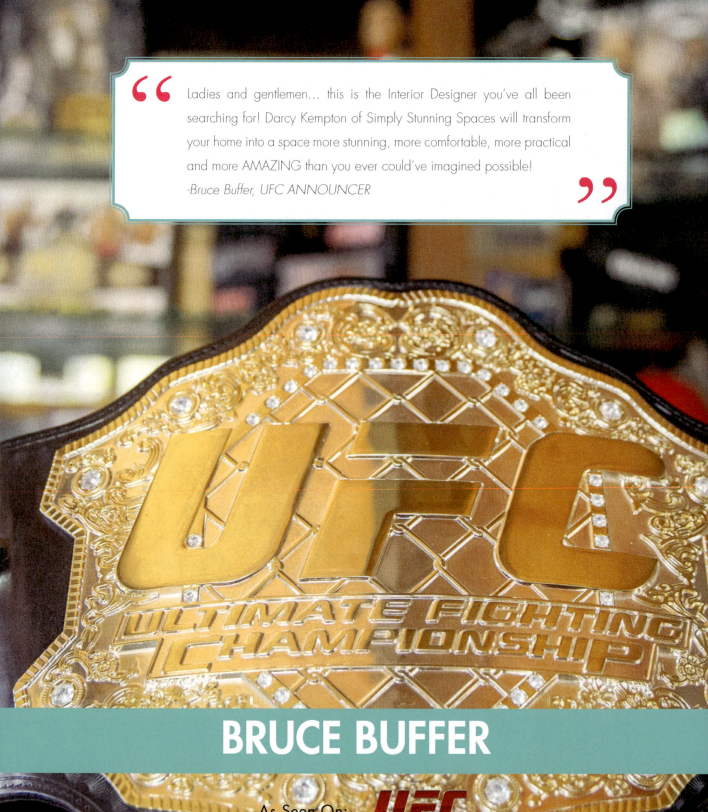

> " Ladies and gentlemen… this is the Interior Designer you've all been searching for! Darcy Kempton of Simply Stunning Spaces will transform your home into a space more stunning, more comfortable, more practical and more AMAZING than you ever could've imagined possible!
> -Bruce Buffer, UFC ANNOUNCER "

BRUCE BUFFER

As Seen On: UFC

MEET OUR CLIENTS

"IT'S TIME!"
UFC ANNOUNCER, BRUCE BUFFER'S HOME MAKEOVER EXPOSED

BIO: The official Octagon announcer for UFC events. On UFC broadcasts, he is introduced as the "Veteran Voice of the Octagon".

MEET OUR CLIENTS

"IT'S TIME!" FOR A HOME MAKEOVER

If HBO Sports called you for an interview, would your home be ready?

Think back to the last time you were planning for a big party. What did you do to prepare? Did you straighten up the cushions on the couch? Hide the clutter? Sweep the floor or do some dusting? Did you buy some new candles?

When HBO Sports called Bruce Buffer and offered to do a special on him and his brother Michael Buffer, with the push of his COO Kristen, Bruce decided to call in a professional to help him get his home ready. The house had to look sharp, and there wasn't much time to pull it off.

I am sure that many of you can relate to Bruce. Bruce has been living in his home for almost fifteen years and, just like most people, he has acquired things. His taste has changed a few times, he has been given things, inherited some things, even made a few bad purchases and his home was looking a little bit neglected and cluttered. Of course he hadn't meant for that to happen, but life sometimes gets in the way, and Bruce had been very busy with traveling and work. Decorating his bachelor pad had fallen to the wayside, but I was ready to step in and help him pull it back together.

MEET OUR CLIENTS

Don't want to give up your old comfy chair? Reupholster it. But don't expect it to be less than buying a new one, that's not always the case.

Switching out your rug can be an easy way to change the look of your room.

Before

40 INSTANT DREAM HOME

MEET OUR CLIENTS

A tip I can give you is to search for treasures in unexpected places. Because of Bruce's love for collectibles I set out to find a unique floor lamp for him. After searching several antique stores through Los Angeles and Orange County I was able to find an amazing floor lamp straight from Walt Disney Productions. Bruce loved the lamp and it fit in perfectly with his home and his style. Searching your local antique stores is a great way to find unique objects for your home and potentially a way to save some money.

ITS TIME!

You never know what you'll find in an antique store. No matter what your style is, go hunting for something original like this Walt Disney Spot Light we used as a floor lamp.

MEET OUR CLIENTS

This poker table converts into a dining table. I love the multi-functional pieces of furniture.

Every dining table needs a chandelier that makes a BIG statement.

Who says dining chairs all need to match? I say they definitely shouldn't all match.

MEET OUR CLIENTS

After assessing Bruce's home and determining his needs and style, I realized that what he wanted was nothing more (or less) than "The Ultimate Bachelor pad Makeover™". His newly appointed home had to incorporate all of his favorite things: his collectibles, his favorite comfy chair, a space for his godsons to feel at home, a tribute to him and his family's history and most importantly it had to feel like a home. It was important to Bruce that the remodel would not take away the warmth that a home gave him and that excited feeling he would get coming back to it after a long trip.

46 INSTANT DREAM HOME

Working around existing furniture can be a challenge, but changing up rugs, pillows, reupholstering & adding a few key elements of design can make a big bang on a conservative budget.

MEET OUR CLIENTS

When Bruce told me HBO could be there in as soon as three weeks I immediately asked him, "What three rooms in your home do you spend the most time in?" These would be the rooms we would focus on.

After discussing with Bruce what he wanted in his home, what his style was and what things were going to stay, we began to make a plan. We decided to start with his office, living room, and outdoor balcony. Along with these focus points, I decided to also make sure to get to the entryway – first impressions are everything.

Bruce has an amazing collection of original, rare and sentimental keepsakes. Every item in his office was a collectible with a story; it was perhaps the most interesting home I have ever decorated. We spent a lot of time going through each item and determining what was most sentimental and deserving of being displayed, what should be listed on eBay, and what should be given away.

Before

48 INSTANT DREAM HOME

Less is more. Be selective with what you choose to showcase, otherwise you risk showcasing nothing.

ITS TIME!

If you're afraid of bold colors inside your home then try them outside first. A little pop of Aqua Blue and you'll instantly feel like you're on vacation.

My favorite outdoor piece of all-time.

Umbrellas are a must for outdoor spaces

Succulents are a great choice for low maintenance plant owners

MEET OUR CLIENTS

ITS TIME!

My team and I gave Bruce a whole new look for his home, all the while keeping a lot of things that he already had and loved. The day before HBO came Bruce and I filmed a video that you can view here: celebritybachelorpads.com. The video will give you a quick overview of his house and some of the things that we were able to do with it.

Think for a moment about what you would do if your house were going to be filmed within the next month. What would you do? Hopefully with the help of my book and the videos that you can view online you would be able to re-amp your home like I did for Bruce. Before you begin, ask yourself these two questions: "What do you want your home to say about you," and "what feelings do you want your home to evoke?"

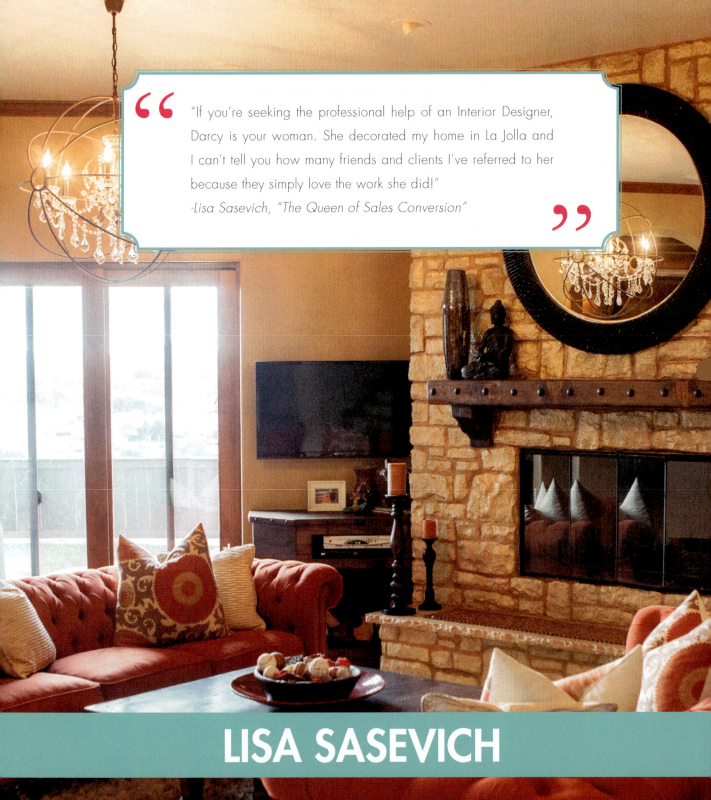

" "If you're seeking the professional help of an Interior Designer, Darcy is your woman. She decorated my home in La Jolla and I can't tell you how many friends and clients I've referred to her because they simply love the work she did!"
-Lisa Sasevich, "The Queen of Sales Conversion" "

LISA SASEVICH

MEET OUR CLIENTS

FIT FOR A QUEEN

"THE QUEEN OF SALES CONVERSION" LETS US INTO HER SASSY CASA

BIO: Lisa Sasevich is one of America's Top Women Mentoring Leaders according to WoW Magazine, she's the recipient of the coveted eWomen Network Foundation Champion award and proud owner of the No. 169 rank on the prestigious Inc. 500 list of America's Fastest Growing Private Companies.

MEET OUR CLIENTS

FIT FOR A QUEEN

"THE QUEEN OF SALES CONVERSION" LETS US INTO HER SASSY CASA

The home was beautiful, and I knew that working with Lisa and her house was going to be a really exciting experience. Lisa had bought the home partially furnished, and with the home already having mahogany floors, rustic ceiling beams, and granite countertops, it already had a good start.

Lisa wasn't in a huge rush to get her house remodeled, which was good because of its size. Because of this, we decided the best thing to do would be to break the decorating process into phases. Phase one was to immediately get anything done that was needed to function with every day life.

Before

56 INSTANT DREAM HOME

FIT FOR A QUEEN

OFFICE

Like many of my entrepreneur clients, the office was an important part of Lisa's home and the room that we would start with. Lisa and her family left on a short weekend getaway and my team and I had only three days to get phase one completed. (Just enough pressure to keep things exciting around here.)

We started with built-in cabinets and wallpaper. The color scheme we decided to go with for her office reflected her branding color, purple. After the cabinets went in and the wallpaper was in place we began arranging furniture. Then, after all of the basics were in place, we dedicated a wall for Lisa's calendars, planning, and masterminding.

There are lots of simple steps that you can take that will make a big difference in your home. For example, Lisa's home was built with beautiful architectural details, but you would never know it because all of the walls were the same off-white color. Painting walls in your home or adding wallpaper can make a huge difference right away, and can make your home seem a little bit more customized to your style. Another great thing that you can do for your home is to go through all of your family photos and get a few of them blown up and framed to hang on your wall. Adding pictures of your loved ones to your walls is one of the simplest and most effective ways to make your house feel like more of a home.

When Lisa returned from her three-day getaway she was astonished by the amount of work that we had gotten done and the huge makeover her office had undergone. For me, there is truly nothing better than a happy client and I was glad that phase one of Lisa's home makeover was such a success. Now, it was time to start phase two.

MEET OUR CLIENTS

FAMILY ROOM

Phase two would be more all-over design. Lisa's home was lacking a designer's touch and held very little personal essence. One of Lisa's focus points was her upstairs family room. The family room was large and open with a slight ocean view. There was a mini bar already in place, plenty of room for seating, and a fireplace.

Although the space held a lot of potential, it was difficult to arrange furniture in a way that would be both visually appealing and useful. Because the room had to be so versatile, I decided to go with a modular sectional that could be easily pulled apart and moved around to create a variety of different arrangements in the room.

To make the room come alive a little bit more we updated the fireplace by faux finishing it in a beautiful Venetian plaster. We then added a custom shelving unit behind the bar, replaced the builder-grade pendants with something that really stood out, and designed floor to ceiling curtains. Lastly, we set out to find some small décor pieces to bring the colors all together.

Before

Before

FIT FOR A QUEEN

MASTER BEDROOM

The next room that I set out to work on was Lisa's bedroom, which held some challenges of its own. The furniture that had been left with the home was beautiful, and likely very expensive, but it didn't fit Lisa's style or the feel of the home.

The furniture was simply too bulky and didn't allow room to move around or function.

In an effort to soften the space while still salvaging as much of the furniture as we could, we kept the existing nightstands but replaced the large masculine bed with a softer, upholstered bed fit-for a queen. New bedding, some color on the walls, new and repositioned wall sconces, accent pillows for the bed and it was presto-change-o.

MEET OUR CLIENTS

KID'S ROOMS

Lisa's kids are absolutely the cutest kids on the planet and I was ecstatic when Lisa told me that she wanted me to make their rooms extra special. When designing the kids' rooms I wanted to keep in mind that their style would change often and tried to make something that they would still appreciate, as they grew older. However, these kids wanted to go wild, and their mother agreed that they would be able to change their room in a few years if it was necessary, so Sierra got a butterfly princess room with butterflies flying from the ceiling and walls. Elijah, her son, wanted to live in a real pirate ship. He had a working ship wheel on his wall that I found on eBay and an old chain ladder that had been refinished at a local nautical antique store, which I then paired with a fisherman's net. I even managed to get an old wine barrel that we used as a nightstand.

Before

FIT FOR A QUEEN

Before

MEET OUR CLIENTS

DINING ROOM

Next up was the dining room. Like in Lisa's bedroom, we were able to keep some of the heavy wood furniture, but also replace some of it with things that softened the room and added color and a new texture. In the dining room we kept the table and side chairs, but we changed out the two captains chairs with something that fit the scale of the room a little bit better and really made a statement. We then added a rug, some accent paint to the walls, and a table setting to tie it all together. Lastly, to make the room feel more open, we uninstalled the bulky shutters to revile the beautiful view.

Before

A PAINT-BY-NUMBERS INTERIOR DESIGN GUIDE 57

MEET OUR CLIENTS

FORMAL LIVING ROOM

The formal living room was a room that Lisa said she hadn't really been using because the sofas were uncomfortable and the room felt uninviting to conversation and family time. Like many of the other rooms in the house, the furniture that came with the home made it feel masculine, dark, and heavy. To fix this, we simply replaced the sofas with two identical light colored tufted fabric sofas (similar to a Restoration Hardware look but for much less.) We also needed to make more of a statement with the fireplace so we set out to faux it with golden highlights and custom-made a mantel that brought some character to the room and really finished it off with the large oversized mirror above it. Then, we focused on the functional aspects that were missing, such as a TV and built–in cabinet to house the components. The coffee table was going to stay, as it was the perfect tie-in with the dinning table in the adjacent room. And, to add a personalized WOW factor to the room we hung a large golden gong. (You'll never miss a dinner call in that house.)

Before

MEET OUR CLIENTS

FIT FOR A QUEEN

Although the cart blanc service that I offered to Lisa may not be for everyone, you can still have the home of your dreams with the help of Simply Stunning Spaces Dream Home-in-a-Box. Our Dream-Home-in-a-Box program follows a similar process and applies many of the same techniques that I used in decorating Lisa's home.

For more information or to book an appointment for a virtual consultation:
www.simplystunningspaces.net   code: Instant Dream Home

Connect with me online for supporting videos at:
simplystunningspaces.net/videos.

> "Darcy's services are really top notch. Thanks to her creativity and resourcefulness we had a beautiful condo fit for entertaining clients and friends in a matter of weeks. I see a lot of products and businesses run across my desk and I'm very impressed with what she has developed with Instant Dream Home. It's a great solution for homeowners and a business model that others could learn from.
>
> *-Mike Koenigs, #1 Best Selling Author, Entrepreneur & CEO of Instant Customer*

MIKE KOENIGS & VIVIAN GLYCK

MEET OUR CLIENTS

BEACHSIDE RETREAT
A SNEAK PEAK INTO MIKE KOENIGS' MODERN ZEN OASIS

BIO: MIKE KOENIGS is a three-time #1 bestselling author, serial entrepreneur, speaker, philanthropist and holds a patent in "Cross-Channel" Marketing Technology. Vivian Glyck is Founder of the Just Like My Child Foundation, empowering women and children in Uganda through Microenterprise.

MEET OUR CLIENTS

BEACHSIDE RETREAT

A SNEAK PEAK INTO MIKE KOENIGS' OASIS

I run into a lot of inspiring people through my line of work and Mike Koenings and Vivian Glycke are certainly two of them. Their work inspires me to be greater and work towards a greater cause. Vivian with her Non-profit organization, Just Like My Child and Mike with his incredible Internet marketing businesses. Together they are an amazing, inspiring couple and I was honored to help them design their new La Jolla condo.

When I met them, Mike and Vivian had just acquired a beautiful new condo on the beach in La Jolla to use as a summer home and for client gatherings. The condo had beautiful ocean views, which was clearly the highlight of the condo. Now, how to make the inside coordinate with that gorgeous view was a challenge I gladly accepted.

BEACHSIDE RETREAT

It all starts with a vision

MEET OUR CLIENTS

Mike and Vivian were looking for a peaceful and fresh Zen atmosphere. To contrast their traditionally decorated primary estate, they wanted something simple, clean, and minimalistic. This is one of my specialties, and I find that a lot of the time simplistic furnishings with just the right accessories and personal touches can make the biggest statement.

The condo was much smaller than Mike and Vivian were used to living in, and having only brought with them their favorite recliner, they were going to need some serious decorating assistance.

Mike is a gadget guy, so naturally the first thing that we addressed was where the television would go. The choice was obvious, because of the beautiful view we wanted the attention of the room to be two-fold. First and foremost, the seating had to be facing the stunning ocean view, but it also had to be comfortable for watching TV as well. A great solution for a dual focal point in a room is to have a sofa with a chaise on one side. This arrangement allows you to only block one side of the room with a sofa back and the other can remain open to the view behind it while still allowing adequate seating for the room.

BEACHSIDE RETREAT

When you're living near the ocean it's hard not to find color inspiration from your beautiful surroundings. For Mike and Vivian's beach house I pulled the beautiful blues of the ocean and sky, coupled it with shades of green and combined them together as a theme throughout the house.

Mirrors are a must-have for small spaces. I am always on the look out for new and interesting mirrors to incorporate into my designs. With Mike and Vivian's beach side home I used a repetition of several mirrors and an array of artwork to make the room feel open and reflect the ocean view. When designing a room keep in mind that the human eye is naturally drawn to items of color so even though your larger pieces may be neutral tones and lacking personality, it's the pops of bold color in accessories, pillows, rugs and art that will make a room really come to life.

When you're struggling with how to make the most out of a small space, consider incorporating multi-functional pieces like coffee tables with ottomans below them, or storage trunks. Oversized media cabinets with wall mounted TVs, and lamp bases that tuck nicely under the sofa are just a few of the ideas we incorporated here. We even found a collapsible dining table that could easily be moved into the living room for business masterminds at the house.

MEET OUR CLIENTS

BEACHSIDE RETREAT

One thing I learned from Mike Koenigs was to never assume your readers know what you want them to do next, so tell them. So, if you want some more tips and tricks on how to get a designer look-for-less then connect with me online at:

www.simplystunningspaces.net

And join our online communities: facebook, youtube, pinterest, houzz, google plus and twitter accounts.

MEET OUR CLIENTS

A DOG'S TAIL NEVER LIES

BEHIND THE SCENES OF A POOCH HOTEL FOR PETCO

ABOUT: These luxury hotels feature spacious play areas, luxury boarding options, and spa services for all types of dogs. They are located in multiple locations across the United States.

SIMPLYSTUNNINGSPACES.NET

MEET OUR CLIENTS

A DOG'S TAIL NEVER LIES

BEHIND THE SCENES OF A POOCH HOTEL FOR PETCO

If you would have told me ten years ago that I would be designing dog hotels for a living I wouldn't have believed you. But now that I have become a part of helping Petco create a luxury brand of doggy daycare facilities I can tell you that it is by far the most fun that I have ever had designing.

Working with Petco has been amazing, and together we have been able to create a program that has become a huge success. I have to say the thing about this project that stands out from all of the others is the creativity it allowed. When working with a home, I stick to certain guidelines and ideas, and although my job always uses creativity, working with Petco to create a luxury doggy daycare certainly pushed my creativity to its fullest.

One of the first locations that really gave me the opportunity to start from scratch was for the Pooch Hotel Santa Monica location. This location hadn't started any construction yet when they brought me onto their team, which meant the sky was the limit. By understanding the price point and target market of the Pooch Hotel customer, I wanted to make sure we appealed to that clientele. Especially being in the posh neighborhood adjacent to the heart of Santa Monica meant this Pooch Hotel needed to ooze luxury. Oozing luxury in my book however doesn't mean making careless expensive selections, no matter what I want to make the smartest selections for my clients.

The first thing I noticed when joining the team was that the color scheme and material selections were lacking that cohesive, luxurious look and feel. Bright colors are great, don't get me wrong but by toning things down a bit and fine-tuning the Pooch Green, we made huge strides.

A DOG'S TAIL NEVER LIES

Suite

STAY RELAX STAY
RELAX INDULGE
RELAX STAY

A DOG'S TAIL NEVER LIES

We combined interior design with graphic design to create a unique vinyl lettered wall. The words "Play", "Stay", "Relax", and "Indulge" helped define Pooch Hotel as a company, capturing the attention of potential customers as they enter.

Waiting Area

Gallery

MEET OUR CLIENTS

For the lobby, we created a customized reception desk by adding detailed patterns to set the mood. Fun filament light pendants balance the space above the desk and incorporate the wood tones from below. We provided our photography service to help customize the space with framed dog portraits along the walls. Later expanding our artistic element to the design with custom screen-printed dog silhouettes that customers can purchase for their home.

Pooch Hotel's play area gave us an exciting opportunity to GO BIG and get really creative. Continuing the exciting design and cohesive branding experience, we used graphic and interior design to make a big statement. Pooch Hotel's "We love dogs" slogan was a large part of their branding, so we wanted to make it big and visible. Originally, the words were smaller and less noticeable from the outside. We utilized the big window from the lobby and placed giant letters spelling "WE LOVE DOGS" high on the walls. Now that is what we call making a statement.

Before

A DOG'S TAIL NEVER LIES

Lobby

MEET OUR CLIENTS

1. 6-foot fire hydrants are now an icon for pooch hotel.
2. The "WE LOVE DOGS" slogan cannot be missed.
3. Play structures keep the dogs' tails wagging.
4. White picket fences make the dogs feel right at home.

A DOG'S TAIL NEVER LIES

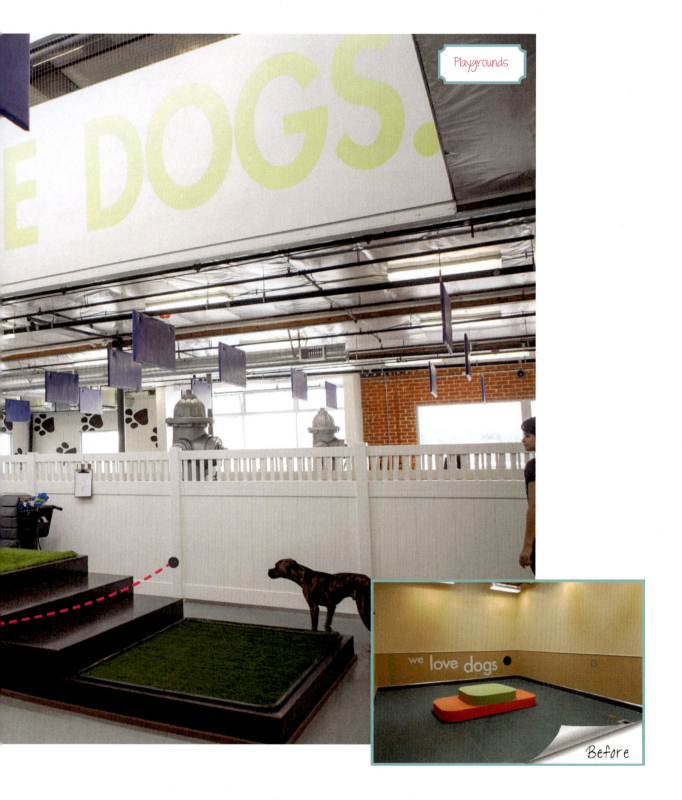

Playgrounds

Before

MEET OUR CLIENTS

We created memorable features in the play area that will keep people talking about Pooch Hotel. You guessed it; it's those giant fire hydrants. These fire hydrants were placed on customized platforms, specifically designed to promote doggie exercise. We also incorporated grass patches into the play structure design for the dogs; so they can feel, well, like a dog. Giant paw prints on the walls define this location as a dog's space.

This was all done with the love of dogs in mind.

Play Area

MEET OUR CLIENTS

At this luxury hotel, the dogs are not just treated to customized play areas with giant fire hydrants. They also get a doggy gym to work out in, a pool to dive into, a salon for grooming and Dog TV™ to keep them entertained when play time is up and the lights go out.

Inside the gym, we utilized both interior design and photography to create a focal wall featuring photographs and tiles to match the space. For dogs who love the water, this is the place to be. Complete with floating toys and lounge chairs, and just for fun we designed a pool rules signage to keep them in check.

Pooch Hotel is now leading the market in the way of full-service luxury dog hotels. With the best staff around, Pooch Hotel even offers web cam service to canine owners for peace of mind when they're away; helping them feel a little less guilty knowing that they're having just as much fun as they are.

For dogs that love water

Doggy fitness center? Heck, Why not?

MEET OUR CLIENTS

Could your place of business use a little design help?

CLOSING THOUGHTS:

1. GO BIG OR GO HOME.
If you can dream it, then it's possible. Don't settle for underwhelming home decor. Get creative, and turn that vision into reality.

2. Make it your own with custom touches. Experiment with painting or photography. Go wild. Just remember to choose a color palate and frame that match your room.

3. Create a conversation piece. This should be something unique that really stands out.

4. Don't forget about the practical application of your design. Buy things that are built to endure daily use.

5. Don't underestimate the power of good lighting. Choose elements that cast light in the right direction without interrupting your design.

6. LOVE the home you are in, and everyone who shares it with you. Demonstrate that love by investing your time and energy into making your home a place you, your family, and guests will love to be.

STEP 1
INSPIRATION

INSPIRATION

Step One in my design process is the fun part, there's no doubt about it. It's all about defining your style through the process of browsing through enough room scenes until you just can't stand it any longer. And then, analyzing and accessing every single one of them in an effort to reveal the hidden design style within you.

Before we dig into all the really fun stuff, I have a few questions I'd like you to ask yourself first.

STEP 1

Completing this evaluation survey is important to help you clarify a few things with yourself before you start wandering off onto your own private distant dream-home design land.

How would you describe your home as it is today? What are the words that describe it? Does it feel cluttered? Does it feel unfinished? Does it feel dark? Does it feel uninviting? Why are you reading this book in the first place? What is it about your home that's really driving you crazy?

Are you just sick of not having enough storage anywhere? Are you frustrated when you can't get comfortable on your sofa? Do you find yourself not inviting guests over for a reason? Do you not have enough places for your friends and family to sit when they come over? Do you have a kitchen that is impossible to cook in? Do you have old flooring that you just can't stand?

Anything that's driving you crazy about the house, big or small, put it down because in your dream home, those things aren't going to bug you anymore. And this isn't about creating a plan that you can do today. We want a long-term plan. But in that long-term plan I want to know how long do you plan to be in this home. Is this a home that you're renting? That you're hoping to be out of in a year? Or is this a home that you plan to live ten or fifteen more years in?

What are three rooms in your home you would most like to see changed? Where do you spend the most time and entertain the most guests? Or where would you entertain and spend the most time if you had the room designed differently?

It's easy to get overwhelmed sometimes with trying to tackle an entire house, so narrowing in on these top three rooms is going to make the entire project seem far more manageable. Once you've tackled these three rooms, the rest is going to be a breeze.

EVALUATION

1. How long do you plan to live in the home you're in? _____

2. Look around... what words would you use to describe your home the way it looks and feels today?
   _____
   _____

3. What words would you use to describe your DREAM HOME?
   _____
   _____

4. How often do you entertain? _____

5. Would you entertain more often if you felt proud to show off your home? _____ If so, what would be the average size of your party?

6. What 3 rooms do you spend the most time in?
   a _____
   b _____
   c _____

7. What 3 rooms frustrate you the most?
   a _____
   b _____
   c _____

8. What would be the most gratifying part about having these three rooms redesigned? How would that make you feel?
   _____
   _____

9. What do you think is hindering you the most from making your home feel like one you truly love? (Time? Money? No direction? No inspiration?)
   _____

10. What part(s) of home improvement or decorating do you enjoy being involved in the most?
    _____
    _____

STEP 1

Big Remodeling Projects are good to plan around, but don't let that stop you from making smaller changes to your home today.

Before

After

INSPIRATION

WHAT 3 ROOMS ARE YOU TACKLING FIRST?

Master Bedroom

Dining Room

Living Room

STEP 1

WHERE TO LOOK

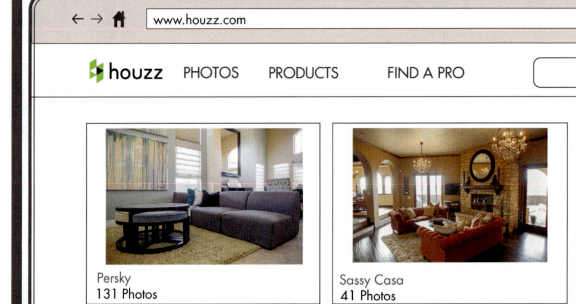

INSPIRATION

EXPLORE HOUZZ

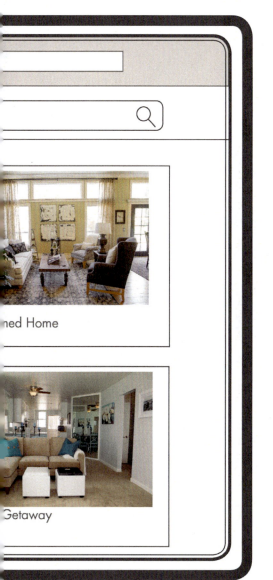

Inspiration can come from the wildest places sometimes. I am always on the hunt for inspiration, everywhere I go. From the restaurants I visit, the stores I shop in and of course the magazines I read and the shows I watch on TV. There's no science or system behind that approach though, so of course there's got to be a better way.

Before I start working with a client, I always ask them to spend some time on houzz.com and do exactly the process I'm about to share with you because one hour of their time on houzz.com is worth a ton of guessing games on my end which saves us both time. I can very quickly get a feel for what kinds of styles I can mix and match with my clients and what color schemes they're drawn to through this process.

STEP 1

WHAT TO LOOK FOR ON HOUZZ:

There are specific questions you should be asking yourself when you are searching on houzz.com. For instance:

WHAT **WOOD FINISHES** WOULD WORK BEST FOR THE FURNITURE IN YOUR HOME?

INSPIRATION

MY DREAM HOME FLOORS ARE:

- ☐ Distressed wood in a wide plank.
- ☐ Mahogany, because it contrasts with my white cabinets.
- ☐ Grey, because it's trendy and beachy.
- ☐ Espresso, because it's timeless.

STEP 1

> **Q**
> WHAT BRIGHT COLORS ARE YOU DRAWN TO?

Cool colors

INSPIRATION

Neutrals

Warm colors

STEP 1

> **Q** WHAT KIND OF PATTERNS DO YOU LIKE?

Tailored Patterns

INSPIRATION

Whimsical Patterns

Floral Patterns

STEP 1

Q
WHAT KIND OF CHAIRS DO YOU LIKE?

Modern

INSPIRATION

Wingback

STEP 1

Q

WHAT STYLE OF SOFAS DO YOU LIKE?

Comfortably Modern

INSPIRATION

Tufted

Tailored

STEP 1

Q
WHAT KIND OF LIGHT FIXTURES DO YOU LIKE?

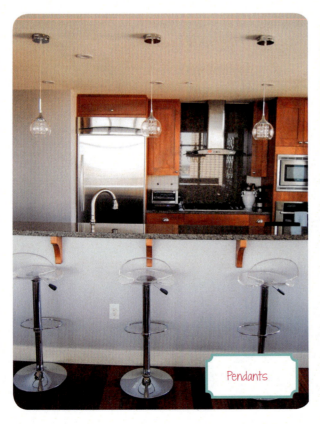

Pendants

Crystal Chandeliers

INSPIRATION

Lamps

Drum Shades

Wall Sconces

STEP 1

Q
WHAT KIND OF **STORAGE** DO YOU NEED?

Sideboard

Media Cabinet

INSPIRATION

Floating Shelves

Built-in storage cabinet

STEP 1

> **Q** WHAT KIND OF **ARTWORK** MAKES YOU FEEL GOOD?

Ocean or landscape

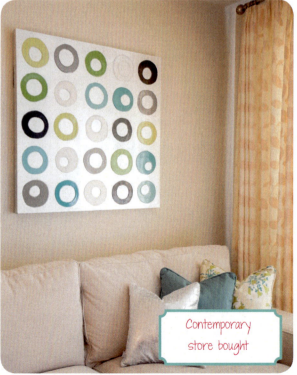

Contemporary store bought

INSPIRATION

Abstract art in just the right colors

Photography

STEP 1

Q
WHAT KIND OF WINDOW TREATMENTS DO YOU NEED?

Shutters because they fit the style of the home

INSPIRATION

Black out curtains for sleeping

Sheer curtains for style

Roller shades for practicality

STEP 1

> **Q**
> WHAT **WOOD FINISHES** WOULD WORK BEST FOR THE FURNITURE IN YOUR HOME?

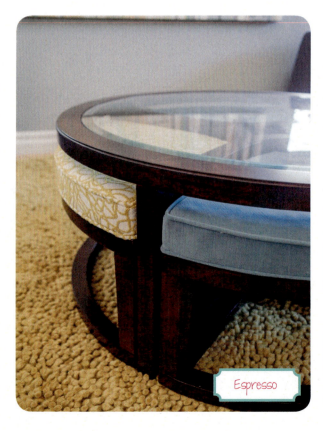

Espresso

Painted

INSPIRATION

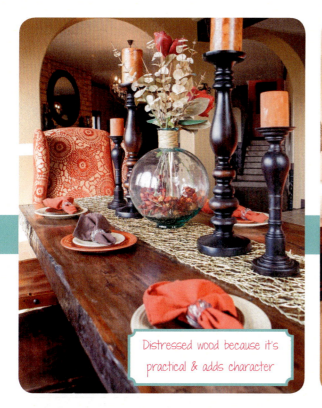

Distressed wood because it's practical & adds character

Mahogany, because it matches my cabinets.

Teak, because it works with what I'm keeping.

STEP 1

> **Q**
> WHAT WOULD YOUR
> ALMIGHTY INSPIRATION PIECE
> LOOK LIKE?

Every single one of my design projects has started with what I call the "Almighty Inspiration Piece". The "Almighty Inspiration Piece" is usually one of three things: a piece of art, a rug or a fabric. It's that simple. It's always one of these for me. Always. If it's artwork, it's usually a piece of artwork that you have in your home already. It's not a piece of artwork that we're going to go looking for necessarily. But if you have a very sentimental piece, a very dominant piece in your home that you definitely want to work around and you can picture it as a focal point in a room; then we want to work around that.

And if you don't have a piece of artwork in your home already, or something sentimental like a rug that you just really love and you've invested a lot of money in, then we need to find that piece.

Visit my Houzz account at www.houzz.com/pro/darcy-k and you'll find 100s of my favorite pieces that I'm just dying to build a design plan around, (or already have).

INSPIRATION

MY ALMIGHTY INSPIRATION PIECE

INSERT A PICTURE OF YOUR ALMIGHTY
INSPIRATION PIECE HERE

STEP 1

CONCLUSION

To stay on track with the Instant Dream Home Process, make sure that by the end of Week 1 you have completed the following tasks:

1. Filled out the SELF EVALUATION form

2. Started an ideabook for each of your Top 3 Rooms on houzz.com

3. Spent at least one hour answering each of the questions in this chapter for each of your Top 3 Rooms.

4. Identified your "Almighty Inspiration Piece".

INSPIRATION

All done?
Then lets move on...

STEP 2
DESIGN PLANNING

TRANSLATING YOUR INSPIRATION INTO
A WELL-DEFINED DESIGN PLAN

STEP 2

DESIGN PLANNING
TRANSLATING YOUR INSPIRATION INTO A WELL-DEFINED DESIGN PLAN

Now that you've spent some time defining the look and feel of your dream home, it's time to take those ideas and translate them into a clearly defined, realistic vision for your home.

It probably wasn't too difficult figuring out what you like, but what's really challenging for most people is figuring out how to take what you love and incorporate that into your home. This is what step two is going to help you discover.

There's a few key elements that make up every single simply stunning spaces design plan.

They are:

1) A SENSIBLE FLOORPLAN
2) A COHESIVE DESIGN SCHEME
3) A SMART BUDGET

A SENSIBLE FLOORPLAN

The first step in creating a sensible floorplan is to take an inventory of what you have, to determine what you would like to use, repurpose or replace. This can seem like an overwhelming task. To make it easier, look at each piece individually, and categorize it as follows:

SORTING

Gather all of your items in one place so you can easily arrange them to see which items work together, which ones don't and which ones could possibly be altered to make them work. When sorting, make four different categories: Keep, Donate, Sell, or Salvage.

DESIGN PLANNING

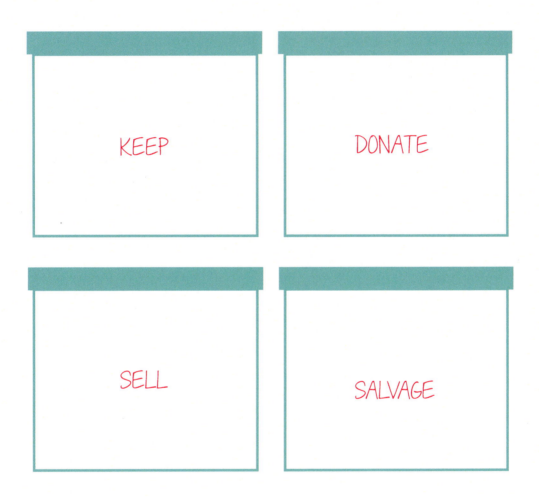

STEP 2

KEEP
Be honest with yourself, do you have a tendency to keep things that probably should have been given away years ago? Do you have a garage filled with things you're going to 'get to'? This step, although hard for many people, is important. Try to only keep the items you absolutely love, are sentimental, and cohesive with your newly defined design style.

SALVAGE
I hate throwing away things as much as most of you and I certainly love to salvage things when possible. This is where your unique style really can come into play. Start looking at some of the items in your home a little differently. Try to imagine them in a different color, a different finish or with a different fabric. A little creativity goes a long way here. A five dollar can of white spray paint to an old mirror with great ornate lines, can come in really handy for creating that shabby chic look. This is a great way to create unique items that you just won't find in the stores. Plus, you can feel good about holding onto grandma's old lamp once it's been jazzed up with a new shade - now a truly unique and personalized item with its own story to tell.

SELL
Sort your list of things you think you can sell and consider these ideas for finding the right buyer. Online classifieds like Craigslist, ebay, consignment stores or yard sales.

DONATE
If you can't sell it, donate it. Here are some great organizations that could use your stuff:

Habitat for Humanity
The Salvation Army
Women's Shelters
Goodwill
Father Joe's

Also, if it didn't sell on craigslist, you can move it to the free section and someone will most likely call you immediately to come pick it up.

DESIGN PLANNING

START WITH THE THINGS YOU HAVE

Start an inventory list with measurements of the things that are most valuable or sentimental to you and take notes here:

Please measure all furniture pieces you have a sentimental attachment to and would like to either (A) Use as is, (B) Re-finish, (C) Re-upholster. *

Room #1: _____

Item A: _____	W_____	H_____	D_____	A☐ B☐ C☐
Item B: _____	W_____	H_____	D_____	A☐ B☐ C☐
Item C: _____	W_____	H_____	D_____	A☐ B☐ C☐
Item D: _____	W_____	H_____	D_____	A☐ B☐ C☐
Item E: _____	W_____	H_____	D_____	A☐ B☐ C☐
Item F: _____	W_____	H_____	D_____	A☐ B☐ C☐
Item G: _____	W_____	H_____	D_____	A☐ B☐ C☐

Room #2: _____

Item A: _____	W_____	H_____	D_____	A☐ B☐ C☐
Item B: _____	W_____	H_____	D_____	A☐ B☐ C☐
Item C: _____	W_____	H_____	D_____	A☐ B☐ C☐
Item D: _____	W_____	H_____	D_____	A☐ B☐ C☐
Item E: _____	W_____	H_____	D_____	A☐ B☐ C☐
Item F: _____	W_____	H_____	D_____	A☐ B☐ C☐
Item G: _____	W_____	H_____	D_____	A☐ B☐ C☐

Room #3: _____

Item A: _____	W_____	H_____	D_____	A☐ B☐ C☐
Item B: _____	W_____	H_____	D_____	A☐ B☐ C☐
Item C: _____	W_____	H_____	D_____	A☐ B☐ C☐
Item D: _____	W_____	H_____	D_____	A☐ B☐ C☐
Item E: _____	W_____	H_____	D_____	A☐ B☐ C☐
Item F: _____	W_____	H_____	D_____	A☐ B☐ C☐
Item G: _____	W_____	H_____	D_____	A☐ B☐ C☐

*Please provide corresponding images, including a close-up, side angle, and & forward facing.

STEP 2

REFURBISH IT

Imagine what your old furniture could look like with a fresh coat of paint or stain & a new fun fabric.

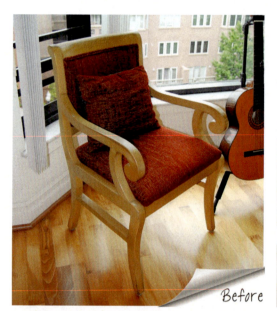
Before

Re-upholster & Re-finish
After

Before

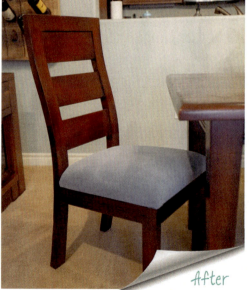
After

DESIGN PLANNING

GATHER YOUR TOOLS

First off, if you have a floorplan of your home, horray for you. If you don't, then I encourage you to take the time to draw one, especially if ordering new furniture is on your list.

The Craftsman electric tape measure is one of my favorite tools. Then of course you're going to need a regular tape measure too. There are a lot of different programs out there that can help you with a floor plan, but first things first; simply copy this graph paper and use it to take down your measurements.

You want to make sure to measure the entire room, including every doorway, window or architectural feature which could affect your space planning. Start by drawing the shape of the room from a bird's eye view. If you were floating on the ceiling looking down at your room, what would it look like? I find the easiest way to get started is at the entrance, so whatever door it is that you walk in, that's where you want to start. You will start your first wall starting at the bottom of the page.

ELECTRIC TAPE MEASURE

TAPE MEASURE

STEP 2

SKETCH & MEASURE YOUR ROOM

On your typical graph paper you want to have one square to equal one foot, so that one little square on your graph paper is one square foot on your layout. Measure every wall drawing the dimensions of your room first. You also want to measure the distance between each corner and the closest window, and then you want to measure the window, and then you want to measure again from the window to the corner. So be as detailed as you can because we want to keep in mind the placement of those windows and doors when we're planning a room.

DESIGN PLANNING

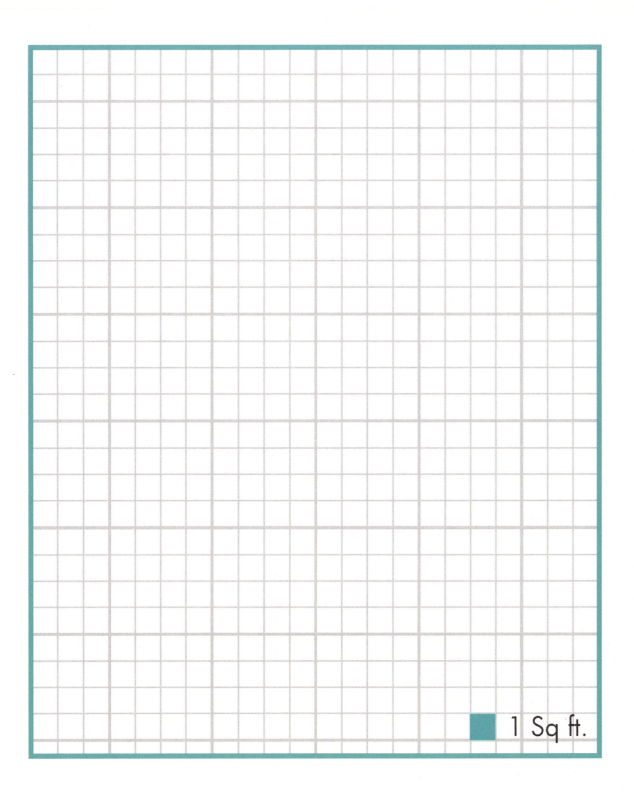

STEP 2

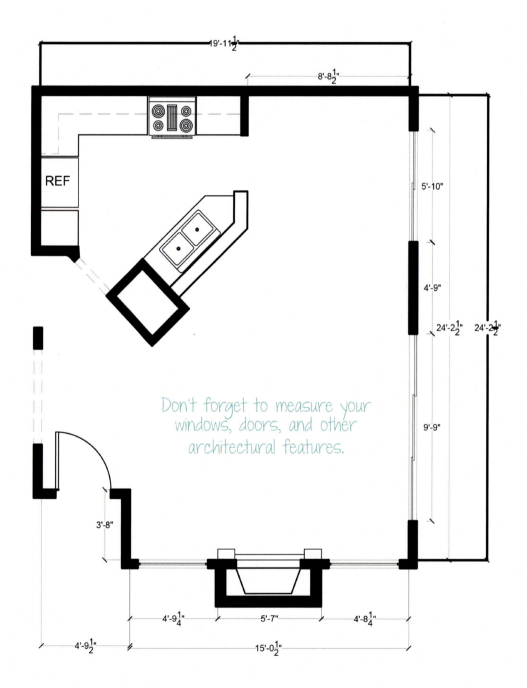

DESIGN PLANNING

For those of you who enjoy tinkering around with new computer programs or apps for your tablet there are a number of options for you to choose from to help you draw a floor plan and experiment with space planning ideas. Here are a few of the ones I have found to be the most user-friendly:

FLOOR PLANNER
Website: Floorplanner.com
App: Floorplanner (IOS and Android)
Price: $9.95/mo.
Benefits: Create and share interactive floorplans online.

HOME STYLER
Website: Homestyler.com
App: Home Styler (IOS & Android)
Price: FREE
Benefits: Creates photo-realistic imagery that captures lighting and textures.

MAGIC PLAN
Website: floorplanner.com/magicplan
App: Magic Plan by Sensopia
Price: FREE
Benefits: Easily create floorplans by taking pictures with your mobile device.

ROOM PLANNER BY CHIEF ARCHITECT
Website: roomplanner.chiefarchitect.com
App: Room Planner by Chief Architect
Price: FREE
Benefits: Visualize your space by physically walking through your model.

PHOTO MEASURES
Website: bigbluepixel.com/photo-measures
App: Photo Measures by Big Blue Pixel Inc.
Price: $6.99
Benefits: Great for adding measurements to your photos.

STEP 2

WHAT MAKES A GOOD SPACE PLAN?

There are a few key things you should understand when trying to design your own space plan.

A FOCAL POINT IS ESSENTIAL

Having a focal point in your room is essential to the overall design. It is your base point from which to plan your placement of furniture. A focal point can be a structural feature like a fireplace or picture window as well as an integral piece, like a television or the bed.

If you're working on a bedroom, typically the bed wall would be your focal point. In a family room, the TV ranks highest as a focal point. It's important to determine the focal point of the room first; this will give you a great starting point for working the furniture items into the space.

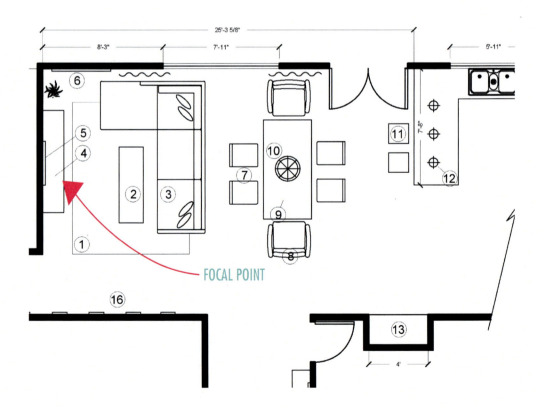

FOCAL POINT

144 INSTANT DREAM HOME

DESIGN PLANNING

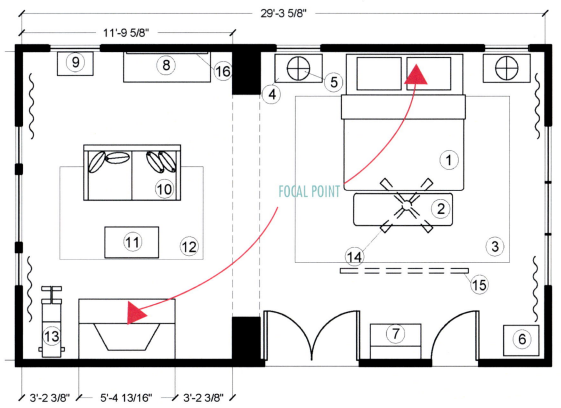

FOCAL POINT

STEP 2

BALANCE IS EVERYTHING

Balance in a room gives it a feeling of equilibrium, which comes from being able to determine the visual weight of objects and how they balance each other through careful distribution. There are two basic ways for creating balance in a room: symmetrical or asymmetrical. Symmetrical balance is the easiest and most commonly used method for creating balance.

Symmetrical balance is fool proof, but can be rather boring. For instance, if you have two dining chairs on one side of the table, you would put the same two chairs on the opposite side of the table and voila.

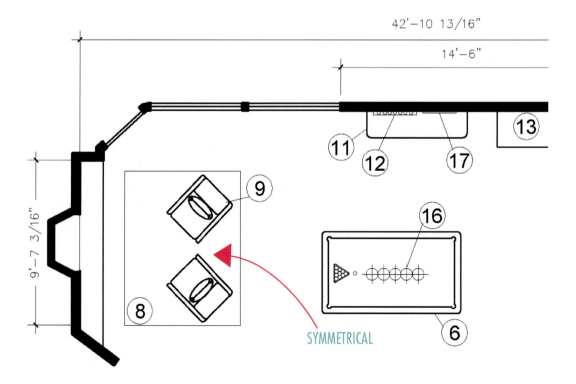

DESIGN PLANNING

Asymmetrical balance on the other hand takes a little more effort and creativity, as well as an eye for what is visually balanced and what is not. I'm here to lend you my "eye". Now, instead of the same two chairs on the opposite side of the table, you could consider a bench instead of the two chairs. Visually this will create a space that is 'heavier' on the side of the table that has two chairs because the chairs are larger, higher and the bench will hardly be seen since it's under the table most of the time. In order to balance this, you could place a sideboard or buffet behind the bench and create a much more balanced room. This is just one example, but with a little practice, you will get the hang of it. When looking at the placement of furnishings, ask yourself; "Is this visually balanced or is it heavier on one side?" If so, then get creative and find a way to balance the room visually.

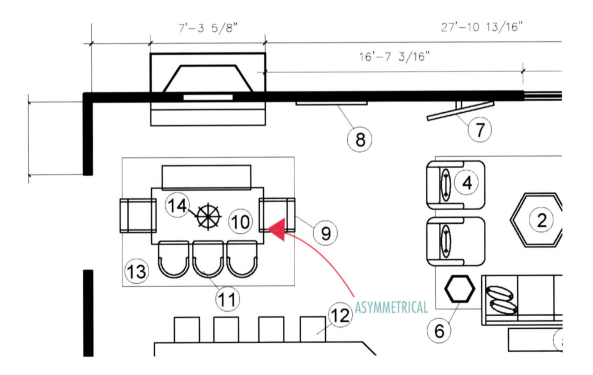

STEP 2

SCALE MATTERS

When something is clearly out of scale in a room it can be one of the most overpowering design flaws. (This is why careful planning is essential.) If an oversized sectional was placed in a small room with little room to walk, you would say that the room is out of scale. Proportion is the ratio between the size of one part to another, and scale is how the size of one object relates to another or to the space in which it is placed. So a large piece of furniture in a small room would be out of scale with the proportions of that room.

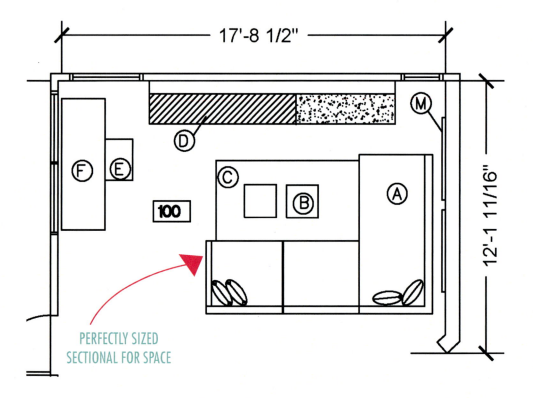

PERFECTLY SIZED SECTIONAL FOR SPACE

DESIGN PLANNING

CREATE FLOW

You've probably heard this word before and maybe you didn't quite get it, but flow is simple with regards to space planning. You simply need adequate space to walk around from door to door and room to room. With respect to open great rooms you want your areas to connect to each other and your furniture pieces to be spaced properly so that nothing feels tight, squished or out of place.

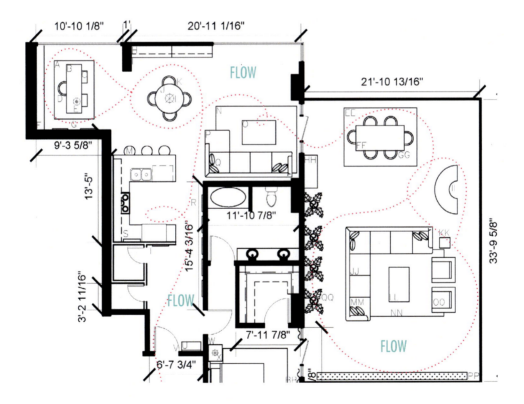

DARCY'S TOP 10 MUST HAVES

1. A GREAT RUG

The first place I usually start.

Consider your rug selection an opportunity to add art to your floors & define your color palette.

STEP 2

Select a rug as your almighty inspiration piece.

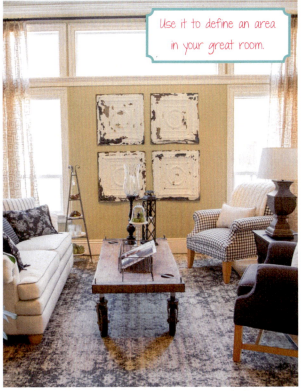

Use it to define an area in your great room.

Bold, shaggy rugs are great when you are putting a rug over carpet.

Outdoor rugs are a great way to add color & personality to your outdoor living space.

DARCY'S TOP 10 MUST HAVES

② ORIGINAL WALL ART

Art is another great place to start when looking for something that will define the colors in your room.

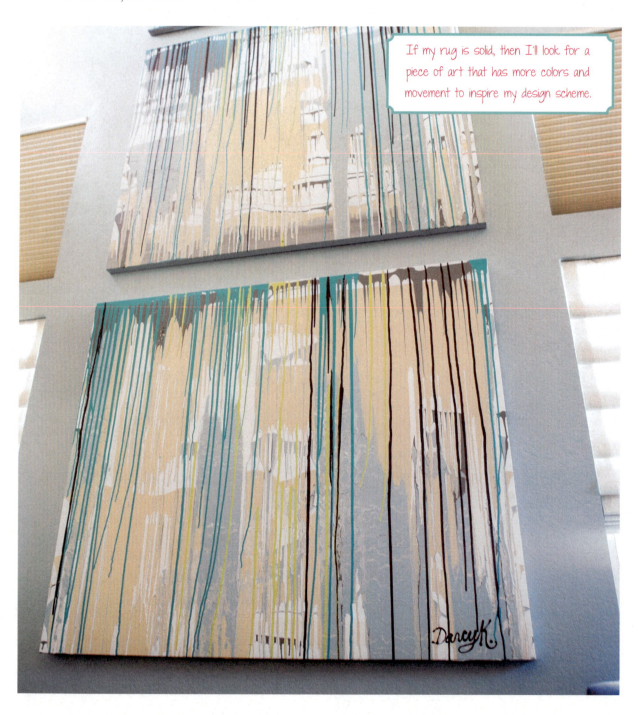

> If my rug is solid, then I'll look for a piece of art that has more colors and movement to inspire my design scheme.

STEP 2

Vinyl art is a great way to make a big pop.

You can't go wrong with black & white photography. The perfect D.I.Y. art solution.

I love buying art when I travel. It reminds me of happy moments & gives me a story to tell.

Want something original? Create it.

DARCY'S TOP 10 MUST HAVES

③ COMFORTABLE, STYLISH & AFFORDABLE FURNITURE THAT FITS

Measure twice, buy once.

This dining set is a combination of an existing dining table, 2 new captains chairs (store bought with re-upholstered backs) and custom seat cushions for the existing chairs.

STEP 2

If it is comfortable, but boring, simply reupholster it.

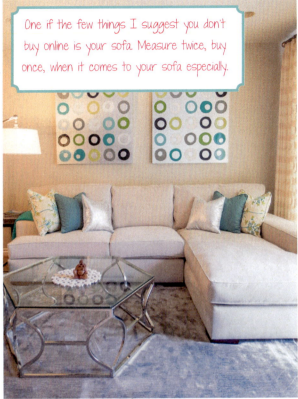

One if the few things I suggest you don't buy online is your sofa. Measure twice, buy once, when it comes to your sofa especially.

Can you believe this bed was only $859 online?

DARCY'S TOP 10 MUST HAVES

4 STORAGE SOLUTIONS

Look for ways to store your stuff stylishly.

Built-ins are a great way to maximize storage

STEP 2

Need more seating? Or a place to rest your feet?

Storage coffee tables are the best.

Sometimes you just have to go custom to truly maximize your space.

DARCY'S TOP 10 MUST HAVES

⑤ STUNNING FABRICS

One of my favorite parts of designing is playing with fabrics. A little bit of splurge can go a long way.

A little paint & a bold, modern print was all this chair needed to earn it's keep.

STEP 2

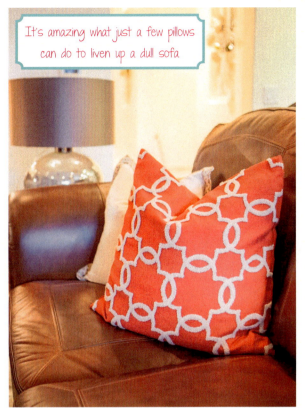

It's amazing what just a few pillows can do to liven up a dull sofa

Combine your patterns with ease. 1 Big, 1 Small.

One of my favorite parts of designing is mixing and matching beautiful fabrics and using them in a way that doesn't break the bank

DARCY'S TOP 10 MUST HAVES

6 STUNNING LIGHT FIXTURES

Say good-bye to your builder-grade light fixtures and say hello to something that really stands out.

The perfect blend of masculine & feminine adds elegance without being too formal.

STEP 2

Floor lamps are a great way to add task lighting.

Free up your nightstands with large pendants.

Don't forget your dimmers. I put them almost everywhere.

DARCY'S TOP 10 MUST HAVES

7 PRACTICAL WINDOW TREATMENTS
Explore your options with a professional.

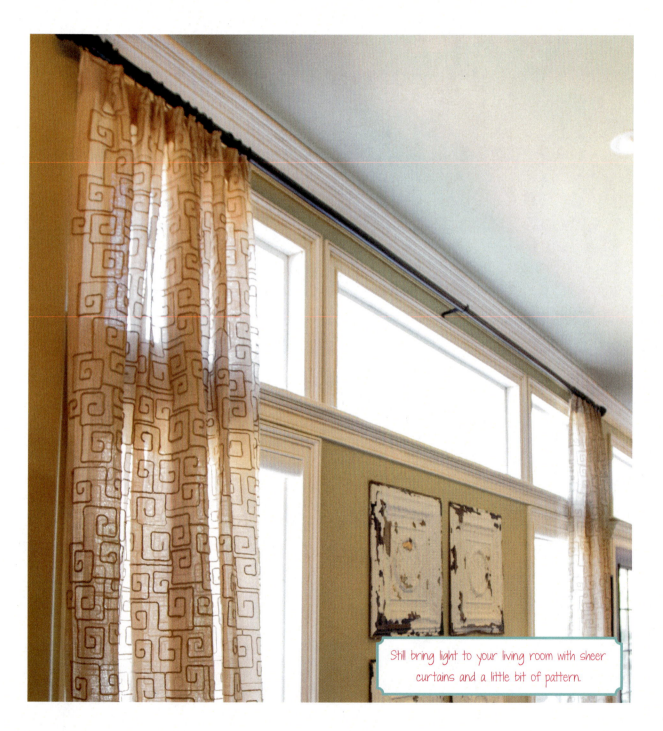

Still bring light to your living room with sheer curtains and a little bit of pattern.

STEP 2

Bring pattern to your craft space with your curtain panels.

Dress your angled windows with custom curtains on a track.

Easy store bought curtains is the most affordable choice.

DARCY'S TOP 10 MUST HAVES

8 ACCESSORIES THAT POP
Sometimes its those little treasures that make the biggest difference.

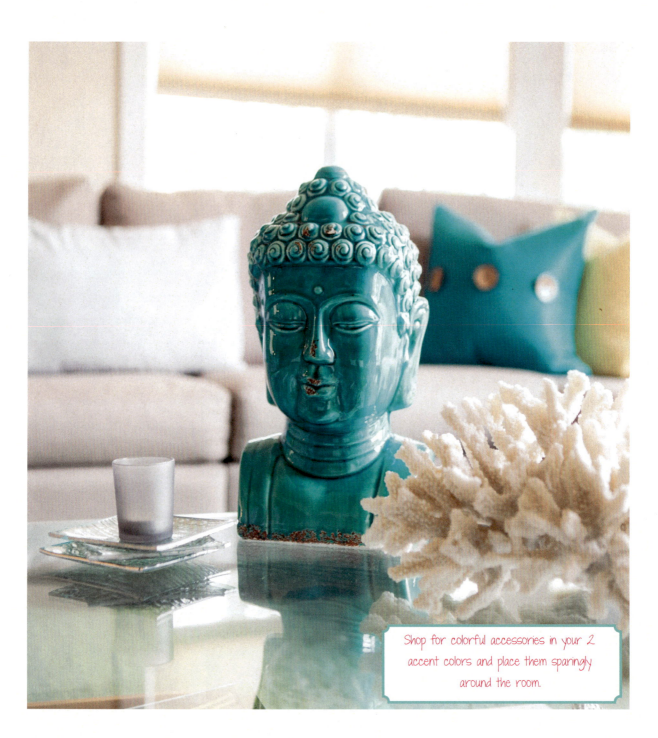

Shop for colorful accessories in your 2 accent colors and place them sparingly around the room.

STEP 2

Dress your plates with colorful napkins.

Toss a bright throw over your modern arm chair.

Placemats are a fun way to bring a pop of color outdoors.

DARCY'S TOP 10 MUST HAVES

9 ELEMENTS OF NATURE

There's a lot more to a room than just what meets the eye.

Plants are proven to increase positive feelings.

STEP 2

Smell: The way a room smells affects your mood. Determine scents you like & burn it in its purest form with essential oils.

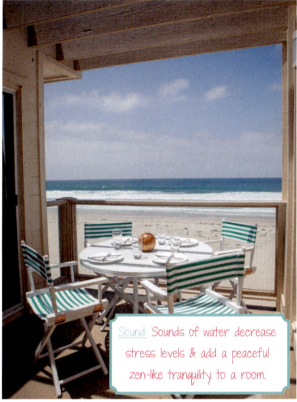

Sound: Sounds of water decrease stress levels & add a peaceful zen-like tranquility to a room.

Touch: I love fuzzy objects. Throw blankets are my favorite way to make sure my clients are comfy & cozy on their sofa.

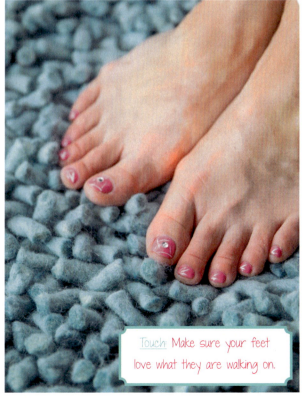

Touch: Make sure your feet love what they are walking on.

DARCY'S TOP 10 MUST HAVES

10 PERFECT PAINT COLORS
LAST BUT CERTAINLY NOT LEAST

The #1 question I get asked most is "what color should I paint my walls?" So, if you're struggling with this one yourself, you're certainly not alone. Good news is, I'm going to share a little secret with you.

Remember that Almighty Inspiration Piece you found in chapter one? Well, that piece is going to determine your entire color palette for your room, and likely your entire home. Why? Because that piece should have only colors in it that you absolutely love. After all, if you love them why wouldn't you want to live with them? Now, do you see why I call it the Almighty Inspiration Piece?

If you are starting to doubt your Almighty Inspiration Piece at all, then now is the time to swap it out. Don't live with hesitation; instead find something you absolutely love.

If you are going to swap it out don't forget that it must have at least three colors in it to be considered the Almighty Inspiration Piece. From here you can determine all of the other fabrics, finishes and paint colors for the home. It's easy now to select fabrics that coordinate with this piece, you simply don't choose anything else in the room, unless first checking it in next to the Almighty Inspiration Piece. Follow this rule: do not waiver and you will end up with a well-coordinated room. My clients continue to amaze themselves at their ability to color-coordinate their room when they follow this simple little tip.

In general, every single room can be categorized into one of the following color categories if it needs to be: rooms are either cool or warm. What do you want your dream home to feel like? Calm and cool? Or warm and cozy?

Generally speaking, cooler color schemes are going to be your blues, greens and neutrals. Warmer color schemes are filled with oranges, reds, and browns or deep plums and terracotta.

Also, I highly suggest never buying a gallon of paint until you have first sampled it on your wall. In order to save yourself from making a big mistake on your wall color, instead I suggest selecting a few color swatches you

STEP 2

think will work and purchasing a small tester or sample size from your local paint store. Once you get home, paint a small square of each color on several different areas in the home where you plan to use this color. Lighting changes from room to room and from daytime to evening so be sure you're happy with the color in both settings before you commit. Also, when sampling be sure to apply two coats so you can be certain this is the color you will be seeing when its completely done.

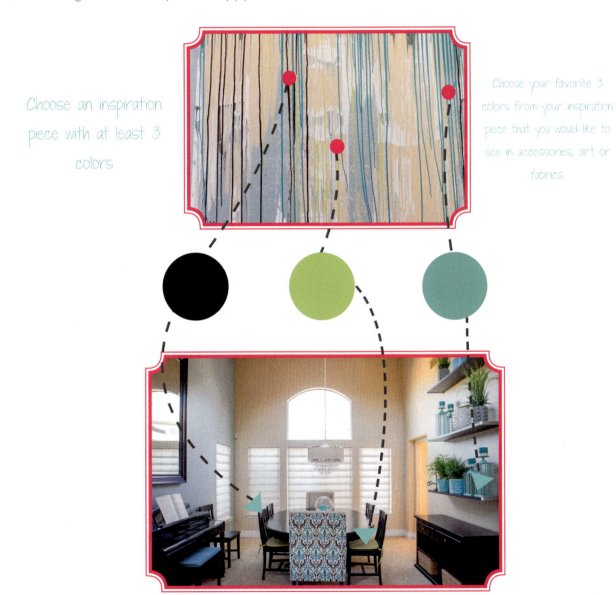

Choose an inspiration piece with at least 3 colors

Choose your favorite 3 colors from your inspiration piece that you would like to see in accessories, art or fabrics.

STEP 2

DEFINE YOUR COLOR PALETTE HERE:

MY ALMIGHTY INSPIRATION PIECE:

{ INSERT PICTURE HERE }

Note: Look for something you already have that you LOVE and want to work the entire room around.

Don't have it? Start searching for a RUG, ART, or FABRIC.

DESIGN PLANNING

MY COLOR PALETTE:

ACCENT COLOR A

{ INSERT PICTURE HERE }

ACCENT COLOR B

{ INSERT PICTURE HERE }

NEUTRAL COLOR

{ INSERT PICTURE HERE }

*Use this color as your overall base wall color

Don't have color swatches to work with? Go to Lowe's or Home Depot and grab them from the paint department.

STEP 2

A SMART BUDGET
Never start shopping without a well-defined budget.
Without a pre-planned budget its easy to get off track and overspend on items where you could've saved. Taking the time to do some careful planning and a lot of research will help assure you're spending your decorating dollars wisely.

Design Budget A			
Kitchen	Projected Cost	**Kitchen**	Projected Cost
Cabinets	$ -	Lighting	$ -
Countertops	$ -	Pantry door	$ -
Backsplash	$ -	Sink, faucet, door hardware	$ -
Appliances	$ -	Barstools	$ -
Total	$ -	Total	$ -
Dining Room	**Projected Cost**	**Family Room**	**Projected Cost**
Chandelier	$ -	Fireplace Tile	$ -
Built-in desk & Countertop	$ -	Built-in cabinet	$ -
Dining table	$ -	Electrical/mount tv	$ -
Dining chairs	$ -		$ -
Window Treatments ALL	$ -		$ -
Total	$ -	Total	$ -
Master Bathroom	**Projected Cost**	**Master Bathroom**	**Projected Cost**
Tub	$ -	Plumbing fixtures	$ -
Cabinets	$ -	Heated Floors	$ -
Countertops	$ -	window treatments	$ -
Flooring	$ -	Plumbing	$ -
Shower & bath tile	$ -		$ -
Mirrors	$ -		$ -
Lighting	$ -		$ -
Total	$ -	Total	$ -
Construction Items	**Projected Cost**	**Don't Forget about…**	**Projected Cost**
Painting	$ -	Furniture Assembly	$ -
	$ -	Trash Removal	$ -
	$ -	Cleaning crew	$ -
	$ -	Shipping & Delivery	$ -
	$ -	Total	$ -
Total	$ -		
		Total Projected Cost	$ -

Fill in the blank with your estimated numbers. Not sure? Do some research online to find average costs for furnishings and fixtures. For construction items start by getting an estimate from a professional contractor.

STEP 2

BUDGET ROAD MAP

CATEGORIZE BY ROOM
Separate your home by rooms and list them in order of priority.

LIST THE ITEMS YOU NEED IN EACH ROOM
Make a list of all the things that each room will need. List out every object you plan to put in the room, make note of the things you already have and the things you will need to purchase.

DESIGN PLANNING

ADD A BUDGET AMOUNT FOR EACH ITEM
Not sure how much things cost? Research online and ask for a contractor to give you a big on your bigger projects.

PRIORITIZE YOUR BUDGET INTO MUST HAVES AND THINGS THAT CAN WAIT
Once you have a better idea of what things cost, start prioritizing and getting creative with how you can make the most out of your decorating budget.

STEP 2

CONCLUSION

By the end of step 2, you should have completed the following homework assignments:

1. Measured your room.

2. Sketched a floorplan.

3. Chosen your inspiration piece.

4. Defined your color palette.

5. Set a budget.

DESIGN PLANNING

Feeling overwhelmed?
Need some one-on-one guidance?

Book a consultation at:
Simplystunningspaces.net

STEP 3
TAKE ACTION
EMBRACE YOUR STRENGTHS, HIRE YOUR WEAKNESSES

STEP 3

TAKE ACTION

EMBRACE YOUR STRENGTHS. HIRE YOUR WEAKNESSES

Now that you've had some time to dig in and start the design process for your home, I'm hopeful that you will have a more clear vision for the color scheme, design style, space plan and overall scope of work for your new home. If so, then the next step for you is to start planning on how you're going to execute these ideas. If you still feel like you're missing some pieces of the puzzle, don't worry because I'll help you fill in those gaps in the pages to follow.

GETTING THE JOB DONE

I'd like to invite you to take a moment and assess your strengths and weaknesses in terms of your D.I.Y. skills. It is important to acknowledge your limitations in terms of what aspects of this design plan you are capable of implementing on your own, and what areas would be best to hire someone else for. Even as a Designer I'm not an expert in every single aspect of home remodeling, I just know how to get the job done.

Getting the job done means hiring people who are skilled in the areas you are not, or who can at least get the job done quicker, better and sometimes even cheaper when you consider what your time is worth.

TAKE ACTION

STEP 3

RANK YOUR DIY SKILLS

Rank your skill-sets for the following common home remodeling and decorating tasks on a scale of 1 to 5 (1=amateur, 5=expert)

1. Selecting the right paint colors for your walls.

       1   2   3   4   5

2. Choosing fabrics, rugs and art that all work well together.

       1   2   3   4   5

3. Purchasing the right furniture for my space.

       1   2   3   4   5

4. Selecting the right lighting for your rooms.

       1   2   3   4   5

5. Installing your own tile.

       1   2   3   4   5

6. Creating your own carpentry pieces.

       1   2   3   4   5

7. Installing new ceiling lights or fans.

       1   2   3   4   5

TAKE ACTION

8. Selecting the right window treatments for your room.

        1   2   3   4   5

9. Staying on budget:

        1   2   3   4   5

10. Hiring the right contractor for the job.

        1   2   3   4   5

11. Finding a bargain deal.

        1   2   3   4   5

12. Creating or finding artwork you love.

        1   2   3   4   5

13. Accessorizing your room with all the little details that make it POP.

        1   2   3   4   5

14. Painting walls.

        1   2   3   4   5

STEP 3

Looking back at the way you answered the previous questions, whom do you think you need to hire to help you complete your dream home? Check all that apply.

☐ A painter?

☐ A handyman?

☐ An electrician?

☐ A carpenter?

☐ A tile installer?

☐ A granite fabricator?

☐ A flooring re-finisher?

☐ A plumber?

☐ A kitchen designer?

☐ A handyman?

☐ A closet organizer?

☐ A wallpaper installer?

☐ A landscaper?

☐ A general contractor?

☐ An Interior Designer perhaps?

GET THE HELP YOU NEED, AT A PRICE YOU CAN AFFORD

Don't panic if the thought of putting all of these pieces together is starting to overwhelm you. Designing your home can be quite the process, and trust me, I know, sometimes you just want to throw your hands in the air and call it quits. Luckily I have developed a plan that can make the process easier to handle. My "Dream Home-in-a-Box" can help you meet all of your immediate challenges and give you a plan that you can start implementing immediately.

WHAT IS "DREAM HOME-IN-A-BOX"?

Dream Home-in-a-Box is a Paint-by-Numbers Interior Design kit for your home. Remember how easy it was to color a beautiful picture in your favorite coloring book? Well this is no different. With Dream Home-in-a-Box you're going to get not only the outline for what your home could look like when it's done, but also a narrowed down list of options for you to consider. Now your furniture, fabrics, lighting, accessories, art, rugs and all of the other aspects of your home will be given to you in three simple choices to help guarantee your success and take away a bit of the headache and frustration that you may be feeling in regards to your home remodeling or decorating project.

HOW DO WE KNOW YOU'RE GOING TO LOVE YOUR DREAM HOME-IN-A-BOX?

If you have followed through the process with me so far, filling out and submitting the assignments I've given you, then I can assure you're going to love the outcome. It's simple really, because by doing this work, I already know what you want, I understand your budget and can work with it so that you don't get in over your head. I have been doing this for years, and nothing makes me happier than a happy client. This may sound cliché, but I started this business not only because it was my passion, but also because I understood how frustrating redecorating your home can be and I wanted to simplify the process. My program allows me to personally help you and understand your needs and wants, which is so different than most of your other options out there. We know how to take what you want and make it all come together.

STEP 3

WHAT IS YOUR NEXT ACTION STEP?

After reading this book, you should either be on your way to scheduling a consultation with me, heading to the store to start purchasing all of the new items for your home, or getting bids from local contractors for your big remodeling project.

If scheduling a design consultation is on your list then YAY. I can't wait to talk to you. It's really simple to book with me, just visit my website: simplystunningspaces.net and click on "BOOK APPOINTMENT". Here you will find all of the options, times and availability to meet with me, either virtually or in your home (for all my local So-Cal neighbors that is).

Wherever you're at in your process it's never too early or too late to call in some help.

TAKE ACTION

CLOSING THOUGHTS

You should have completed the following assignments:

1 Created an orderly "TO-DO" list.

2 Delegated someone to each item on the TO-DO list.

3 Received referrals & bids for the big items on your list.

Your dream home is right around the corner! All you need to do is take action (any action) Today!

CASE STUDY

IF THEY CAN DO IT, SO CAN YOU.

CASE STUDY

CASE STUDY:

The Persky family residence is the perfect example of what is possible for you and your home.

Before

CASE STUDY

After

CASE STUDY

1 INITIAL CONSULTATION

The first thing Kelly Persky did was booked an appointment with me on my website: simplystunningspaces.net. She conveniently chose to meet over facetime where we spent about an hour going through my initial survey, analyzing her needs and discussing some general design ideas.

VIRTUAL CONSULTATION

CHOOSE THE ONE YOUR ARE MOST FAMILIAR WITH

CASE STUDY

CASE STUDY

 HOUZZ IDEABOOK

IDEABOOK

One of the first things we ask our clients to do is create an ideabook on Houzz.com. Here you can see a small sample of the images and notes that Kelly gave us to help clearly define her style.

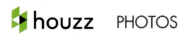

Fabric on the end chairs

I want to stain my floors!

CASE STUDY

FIND A PRO

Wall Color

Color Scheme

Chandelier

I like the mirror

CASE STUDY

③ EVALUATION

1. How long do you plan to live in the home you're in?
   5 or more years, than we plan to move to our condo.

2. Look around... what words would you use to describe your home the way it looks and feels today?
   Outdated, not cohesive. My style has changed since we moved in 14 years ago.

3. What words would you use to describe your DREAM HOME?
   I just want to live in a beautiful, clean, efficient, low maintenance, visually pleasing (but love & groovy) space.

4. How often do you entertain? _once/month_

5. Would you entertain more often if you felt proud to show off your home? _probably_ If so, what would be the average size of your party?: _6_ maximum size? _15-20_

6. What 3 rooms do you spend the most time in?
   a _Family room_
   b _Kitchen_
   c _Living room_

7. What 3 rooms frustrate you the most?
   a _Kitchen_
   b _Family room_
   c _Living room/ Dining room_

8. What would be the most gratifying part about having these three rooms redesigned? How would that make you feel?
   I cool a lot less than I used to, but I think I would do more of it if my kitchen was updated.
   I love having friends and family over.

9. What do you think is hindering you the most from making your home feel like one you truly love? (Time? Money? No direction? No inspiration?)
   I used to love decorating, but I just dont have the time or energy anymore.

10. What part(s) of home improvement or decorating do you enjoy being involved in the most?
    I enjoy decorating, but I know my limits.

CASE STUDY

There are a series of questions that are important to get answers to when starting with a new client. We needed to assess and prioritize the Persky's needs before we could start doing any design planning. We also needed an inventory list, pictures, and measurements of all the items in the home they wanted us to consider using or re-purposing.

FURNITURE INVENTORY

Please measure all furniture pieces you have a sentimental attachment to and would like to either (A) Use as is, (B) Re-finish, (C) Re-upholster. *

Room #1: Formal Dining Room

Item A: Dining table	W 82	H 30	D 60	A[X] B[X] C[X]
Item B: Dining chairs	W 18	H 18	D 18	A[X] B[X] C[X]
Item C: Piano	W	H	D	A[X] B[ ] C[ ]
Item D: Mirror	W 45	H	D	A[ ] B[ ] C[X]
Item E:	W	H	D	A[ ] B[ ] C[ ]
Item F:	W	H	D	A[ ] B[ ] C[ ]
Item G:	W	H	D	A[ ] B[ ] C[ ]

Room #2: Living Room

Item A: Sectional	W 113	H 19	D 113	A[X] B[ ] C[ ]
Item B:	W	H	D	A[ ] B[ ] C[ ]
Item C:	W	H	D	A[ ] B[ ] C[ ]
Item D:	W	H	D	A[ ] B[ ] C[ ]
Item E:	W	H	D	A[ ] B[ ] C[ ]
Item F:	W	H	D	A[ ] B[ ] C[ ]
Item G:	W	H	D	A[ ] B[ ] C[ ]

Room #3: Family Room & Kitchen

Item A: Ann Sacs tile clear	W 33 SQ ft	H	D	A[X] B[ ] C[ ]
Item B: Ann Sacs tile black	W 6 SQ ft	H	D	A[X] B[ ] C[ ]
Item C:	W	H	D	A[ ] B[ ] C[ ]
Item D:	W	H	D	A[ ] B[ ] C[ ]
Item E:	W	H	D	A[ ] B[ ] C[ ]
Item F:	W	H	D	A[ ] B[ ] C[ ]
Item G:	W	H	D	A[ ] B[ ] C[ ]

*Please provide corresponding images, including a close-up, side angle, and & forward facing.

CASE STUDY

Pictures, Video & Measurements complete the list of items we need to begin a new project.

BEFORE PICTURES

CASE STUDY

FLOOR PLAN SKETCH OF ALL 3 ROOMS

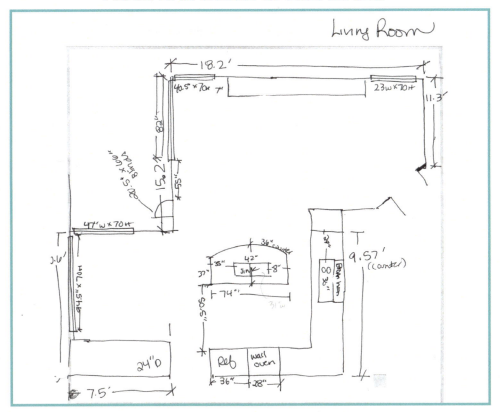

YOUTUBE VIDEO

CASE STUDY

4 DESIGN REVEAL

2-3 weeks later, the Persky's design presentation was ready to be viewed online, complete with 3D computer renderings, floor plans, purchasing information for every item in the design plan, budget spreadsheet, list of priorities, step-by-step instructions and recommendations for implementation.

CASE STUDY

CASE STUDY

5️⃣ INTERIOR DESIGN KIT

DESIGN WORKBOOK

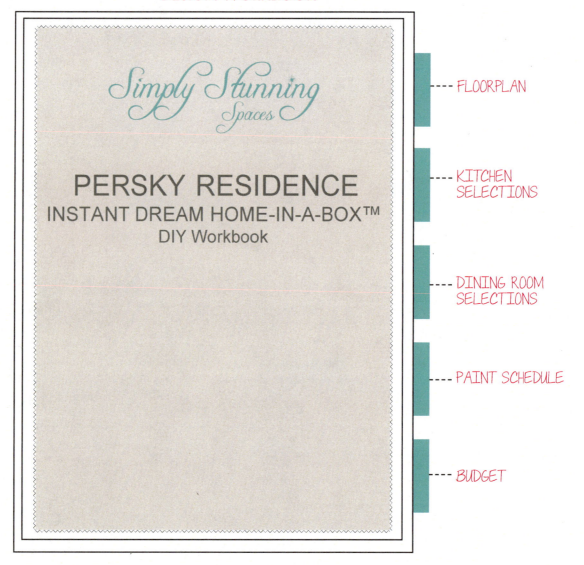

- FLOORPLAN
- KITCHEN SELECTIONS
- DINING ROOM SELECTIONS
- PAINT SCHEDULE
- BUDGET

The design workbook is one of the most important pieces of the design kit. In the Persky's workbook there were floor plans, kitchen selections, dining room selections, a paint schedule, and information about their budget.

CASE STUDY

 ## COMPUTER RENDERINGS

The Perskys wanted to focus on their kitchen, family room, living room, formal dining room and guest bedroom. In their design kit we included renderings for each of these areas.

FAMILY ROOM & KITCHEN

FORMAL LIVING & DINING

CASE STUDY

PAINT-BY-NUMBERS DECISION-MAKING
We help you fill in the blanks.

7 FAN
Brand:_____
Item#:_____

8 WALL DECOR
Brand:_____
Item#:_____

6 WINDOW TREATMENTS
Brand:_____
Item#:_____

5 NEW TV
Brand:_____
Item#:_____

4 RUG
Brand:_____
Item#:_____

4 FIREPLACE TILE
Brand:_____
Item#:_____

3 PAINTED MANTEL
Painted mantel color:_____

2 PAINTED CABINET
Color:_____

1 HEARTH
Brand:_____
Item#:_____

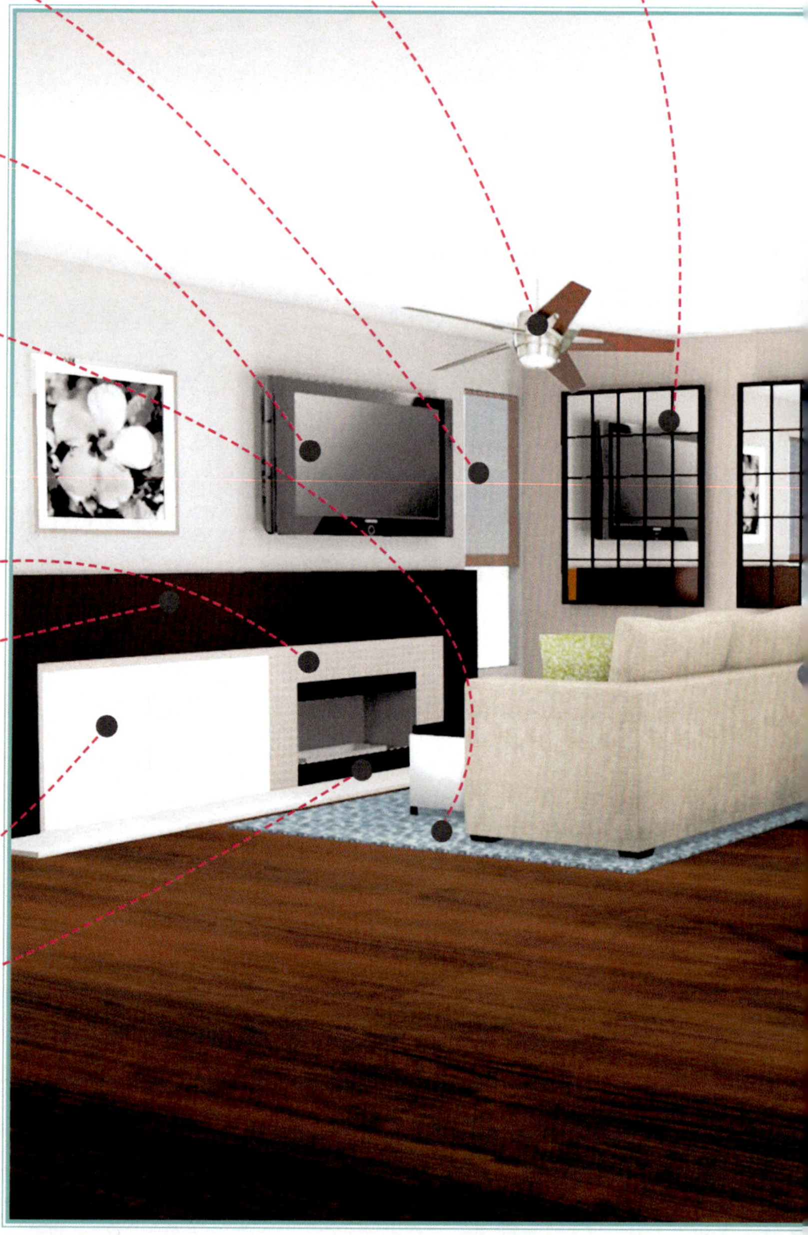

206 INSTANT DREAM HOME

CASE STUDY

9 LIGHT FIXTURES
Brand:_____
Item#:_____

10 HARDWARE
Brand:_____
Item#:_____

11 BACKSPLASH
Brand:_____
Item#:_____

12 COOKTOP
Brand:_____
Item#:_____

13 CABINETS
Paint:_____
Color:_____

14 COUNTER TOP
Material:_____

15 SINK
Brand:_____
Item#:_____

16 BARSTOOLS
Brand:_____
Item#:_____

17 FLOORS
Stain color:_____

Before

CASE STUDY

 ## PURCHASING INFORMATION

The Perskys now had an idea of what their new home was going to look like, but we didn't want to leave them in the dark or scrambling with trying to figure out what to do next. In this section of the design kit the Perskys were given information about each piece of furniture that they needed to purchase. Included in this information was where the piece could be purchased, what its dimensions were, its price and quantity, and if any discount was offered on it.

Room: Dining Room

Items: Dining Chairs

Item Description: Becca Nailhead Dining Chair
Nailhead Dining Chairs Offer Elegance for the Dining Room or Office

Item # : 08452

Color: Natural linen and blue/grey

Dimensions: 36"H X22"W
Quantity:2

Price: $199.00

Vendor: Home decorators

Link: http://www.homedecorators.com/P/Becca_Nailhead_Dining_Chair/830/

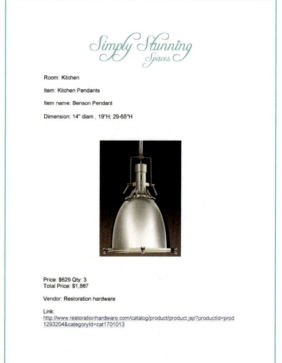

Room: Kitchen

Item: Kitchen Pendants

Item name: Benson Pendant

Dimension: 14" diam , 19"H; 29-65"H

Price: $629 Qty: 3
Total Price: $1,887

Vendor: Restoration hardware

Link:
http://www.restorationhardware.com/catalog/product/product.jsp?productId=prod1293204&categoryId=cat1701013

ITEMIZED BUDGET

As my team and I decided on what pieces of furniture to add to Kelly's home we made sure to stay in her budget. We gave her a variety of different options for each piece, letting her make the decision about where she wanted to splurge and where she wanted to save.

As you can see from the table bellow the items were separated by the rooms that they would be placed in. By doing this, Kelly was able to better see where each piece would go and what its role would be, which would help her make decisions.

Design Budget A			
Kitchen	**Projected Cost**	**Living Room**	**Projected Cost**
Pendant lights	$ 900	IR emiter	$ 150
Barstools	$ 900	New shelf for ent. Unit	$ 350
Install new faucet & Sink	$ 350		$ -
Construction Bid	$ 21,331		$ -
(Refinish cabinets, floors,	$ -		$ -
Fireplace Remodel, cooktop.	$ -		$ -
Electrical.)	$ -		$ -
	$ -		
Total	**$ 23,481**	**Total**	**$ 500**
Guest Room	**Projected Cost**	**Bfast Nook**	**Projected Cost**
Sofa Bed	$ 1,500	Dining table	$ 700
Desk set up	$ 675	Rug	$ 500
Nightstand	$ 350	Dining chairs	$ 1,000
lamp/mirror & pillows/light	$ 900		$ -
Curtains	$ 400		$ -
Total	**$ 3,825**	**Total**	**$ 2,200**

CASE STUDY

6 THE END RESULT

"Darcy, I can't tell you how much we enjoy the new downstairs space you helped us create. It "feels" so much better than before and we hope we can achieve a similar feeling upstairs with your guidance."
-Bill & Kelly Persky

Before

CASE STUDY

CASE STUDY

A FEW SMART CHANGES & COST-EFFECTIVE

UPDATES CAN MAKE A BIG DIFFERENCE

Before

Practical window treatments

Space for every day life

212 INSTANT DREAM HOME

CASE STUDY

Comfortable furniture

Efficient stylish lighting

Smart storage solutions

CASE STUDY

Make it feel like the
dream home
you have always wanted.

Art that speaks to you

Before

CASE STUDY

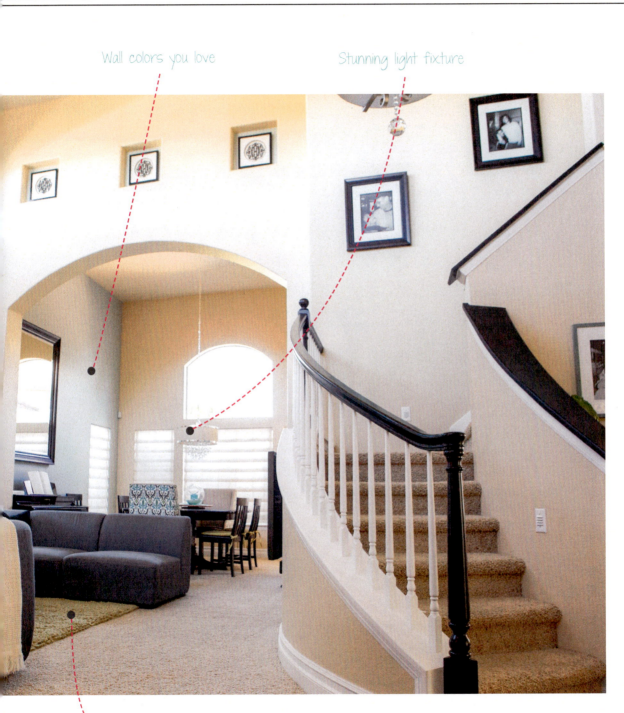

Wall colors you love

Stunning light fixture

A rug that feels good on your feet

CASE STUDY

CASE STUDY

Curious to know what your Dream Home-in-a-Box would look like?

Let us help to take the headache out of decorating for you and make it as simple as 1-2-3.

1. Start an ideabook

2. Complete evaluation

3. Schedule your initial consultation online at:

Simplystunningspaces.net

Click "Book Appointment"

IMAGINE THE POSSIBILITIES

PAINT-BY-NUMBERS DECORATING

WHAT IF DECORATING YOUR HOME WAS AS EASY AS PAINT-BY-NUMBERS?

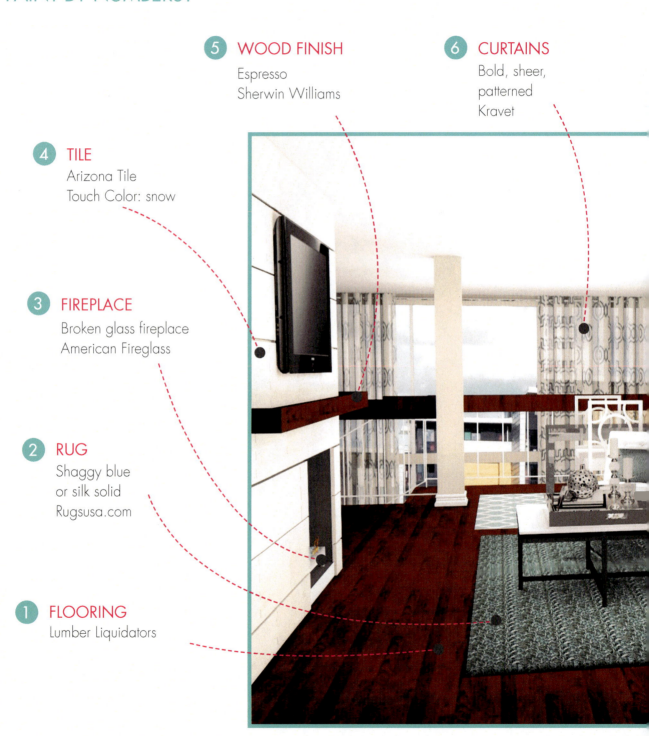

5 WOOD FINISH
Espresso
Sherwin Williams

6 CURTAINS
Bold, sheer, patterned
Kravet

4 TILE
Arizona Tile
Touch Color: snow

3 FIREPLACE
Broken glass fireplace
American Fireglass

2 RUG
Shaggy blue or silk solid
Rugsusa.com

1 FLOORING
Lumber Liquidators

IMAGE THE POSSIBILITIES

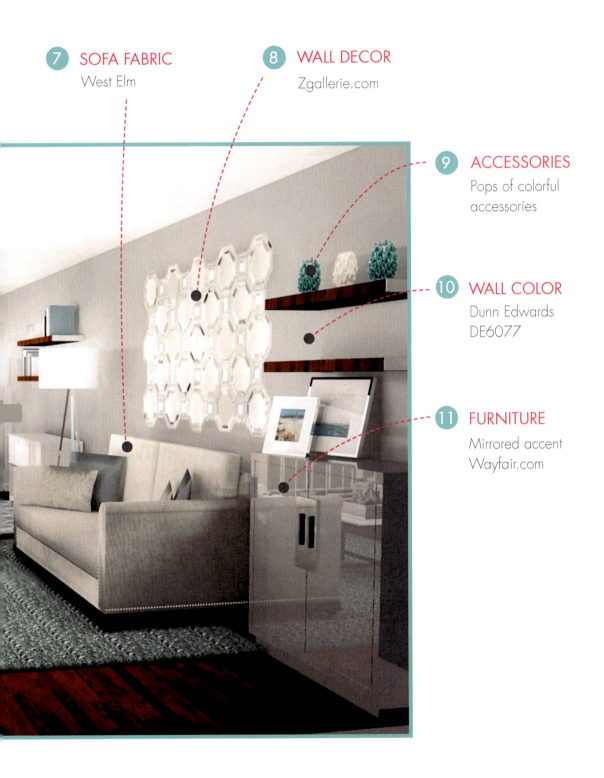

7 SOFA FABRIC
West Elm

8 WALL DECOR
Zgallerie.com

9 ACCESSORIES
Pops of colorful accessories

10 WALL COLOR
Dunn Edwards
DE6077

11 FURNITURE
Mirrored accent
Wayfair.com

PAINT-BY-NUMBERS DECORATING

WHAT IF YOU KNEW EXACTLY WHERE TO BUY EVERYTHING YOU NEEDED FOR YOUR HOME?

4 MANTEL
Painted
Sherwin Williams

5 TV
Wall mount
Bestbuy.com

3 FIREPLACE TILE
New mosaic fireplace tile
Arizona Tile

2 BARSTOOLS
Overstock.com

1 BAR
Keep simple
All parts IKEA.com

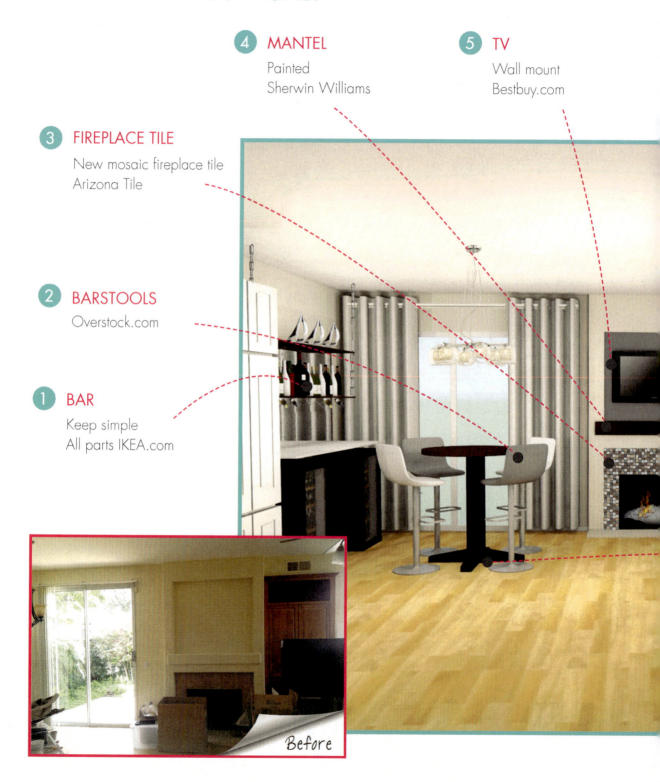

Before

IMAGINE THE POSSIBILITIES

6 FURNITURE
White painted cabinets
Sherwin Williams

7 ART
Custom made photo art
Istockphoto.com

8 STORAGE
Storage ottomans helps in small spaces
Crateandbarrel.com

9 CURTAINS
Should always replace vertical blinds
Bedbathandbeyond.com

10 BAR HEIGHT TABLE
With alternating dual toned barstools
Wayfair.com

PAINT-BY-NUMBERS DECORATING

HOW MUCH TIME & MONEY COULD YOU SAVE?

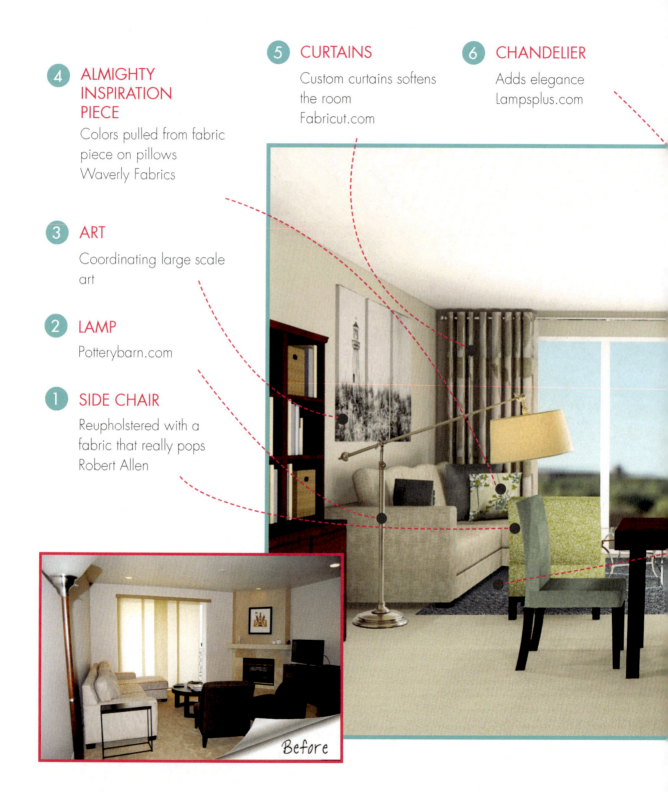

5 CURTAINS
Custom curtains softens the room
Fabricut.com

6 CHANDELIER
Adds elegance
Lampsplus.com

4 ALMIGHTY INSPIRATION PIECE
Colors pulled from fabric piece on pillows
Waverly Fabrics

3 ART
Coordinating large scale art

2 LAMP
Potterybarn.com

1 SIDE CHAIR
Reupholstered with a fabric that really pops
Robert Allen

Before

IMAGINE THE POSSIBILITIES

7 FOCAL POINT
Gives opportunity for accent paint

8 WOOD
New mantel to match dining table
Sherwin Williams

9 TILE
Retiled crushed gloss 2x2 tile
Oceanside Glass

10 MIRROR
Enlarges and brightens the space
Zgallerie.com

11 RUG
Blue silk rug adds color & refines the spaces
Stunningrugs.com

12 DINING CHAIRS
Reupholstered seats in blue velvet
Macys.com

PAINT-BY-NUMBERS DECORATING

WHAT IS YOUR HOME'S TRUE POTENTIAL?

5 ACCESSORIES
Potterybarn.com

4 CURTAIN ROD
Custom sheer draperies
Restoration Hardware

3 STONE WALL
Add texture
Eldorado Stone

2 PILLOWS
Zgallerie.com

1 FLOOR LAMP
Potterybarn.com

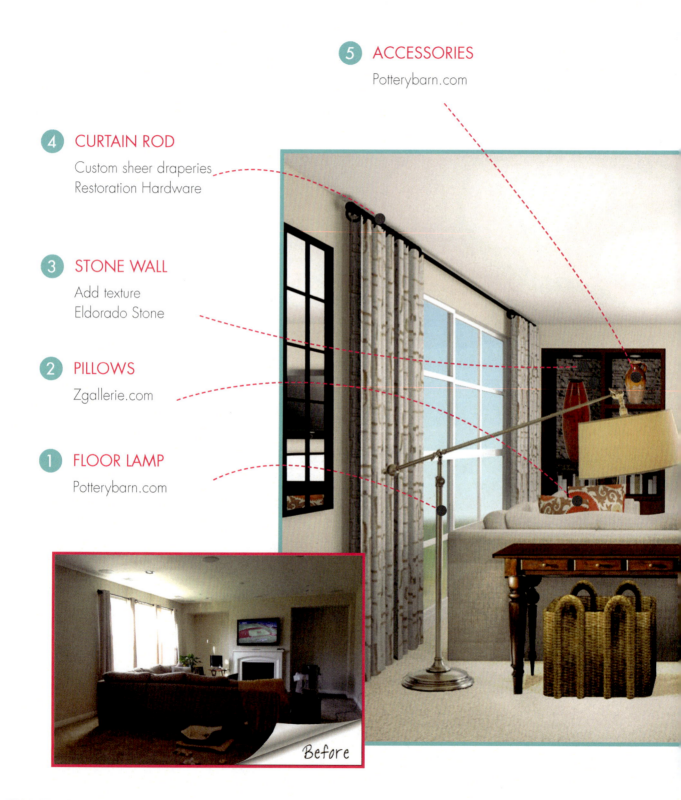

Before

226 INSTANT DREAM HOME

IMAGINE THE POSSIBILITIES

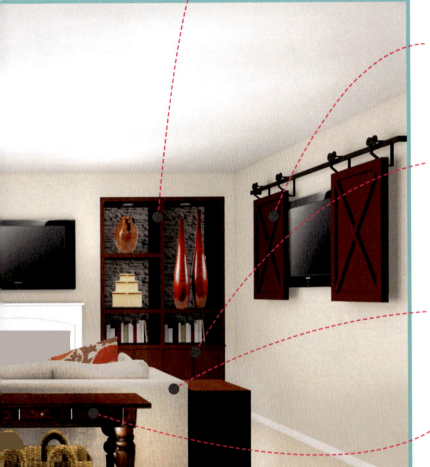

6 BUILT-IN
Creative, practical carpentry design for empty niches

7 HIDDEN TV
A creative solution to the request for a 2nd TV in the room
Potterybarn.com

8 TV COMPONENTS
Hide your TV components with the use of an I.R. emitter
Frys.com

9 SOFA
Macys.com

10 CONSOLE TABLE & BASKETS
Disguise the back of the sofa
Potterybarn.com

PAINT-BY-NUMBERS DECORATING

HOW COULD YOUR BUSINESS OR OFFICE BENEFIT FROM A SERVICE LIKE THIS?

5 WALL ART
Vintage B&W Photography by Local Artists

6 CEILING
Reveal exposed beams

4 TABLES
Custom-made GluLam Beam tables

3 BOOTH BACK
Robert Allen Contract Fabric

2 BOOTH SEAT
Robert Allen vinyl seat

1 BARSTOOLS
Restoration Hardware

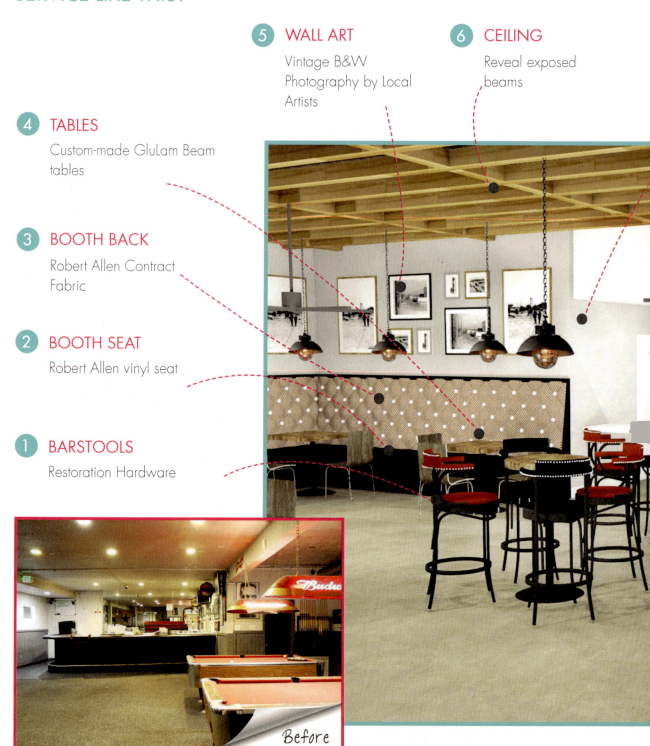

Before

IMAGINE THE POSSIBILITIES

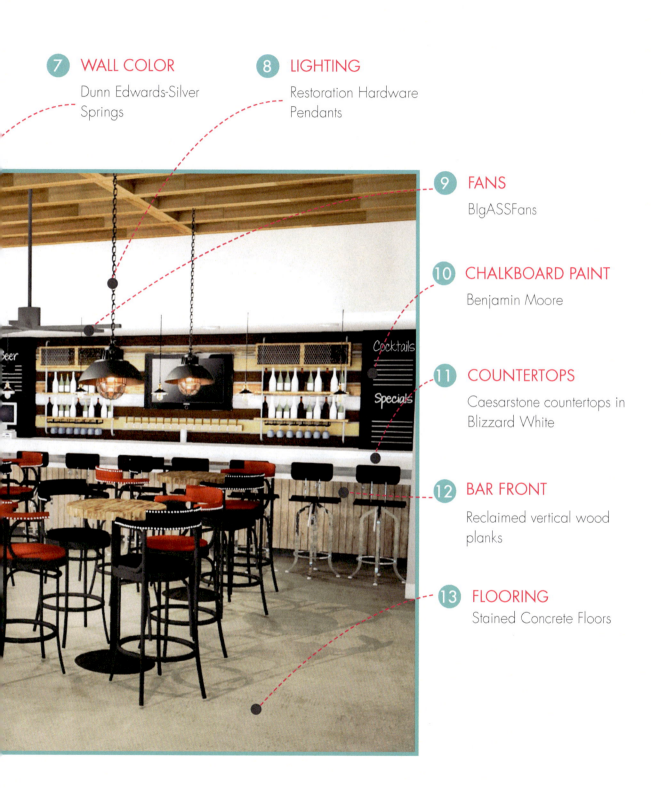

7 WALL COLOR
Dunn Edwards-Silver Springs

8 LIGHTING
Restoration Hardware Pendants

9 FANS
BIgASSFans

10 CHALKBOARD PAINT
Benjamin Moore

11 COUNTERTOPS
Caesarstone countertops in Blizzard White

12 BAR FRONT
Reclaimed vertical wood planks

13 FLOORING
Stained Concrete Floors

PAINT-BY-NUMBERS DECORATING

NOT JUST FOR HOMES, WE DO BUSINESSES, HOTELS & RESTAURANTS TOO.

④ PAINT COLOR A
Dunn Edwards, Shining Knight

⑤ PAINT COLOR B
Dunn Edwards Sparkling Frost

③ BASEBOARDS
6" Baseboards, Home Depot painted in Dunn Edwards Igloo

② COUNTERTOPS
Silestone Kensho

① CABINETRY
White Shaker Style Cabinet Doors

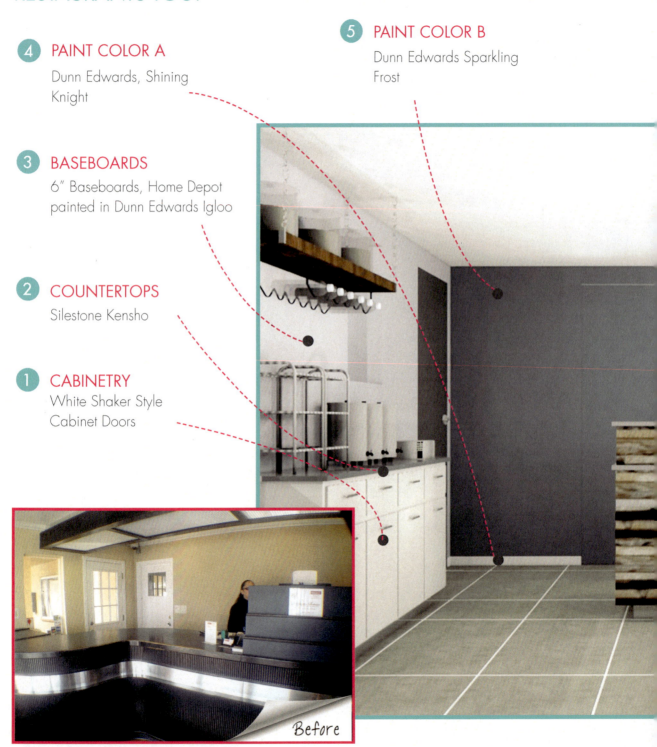

Before

IMAGE THE POSSIBILITIES

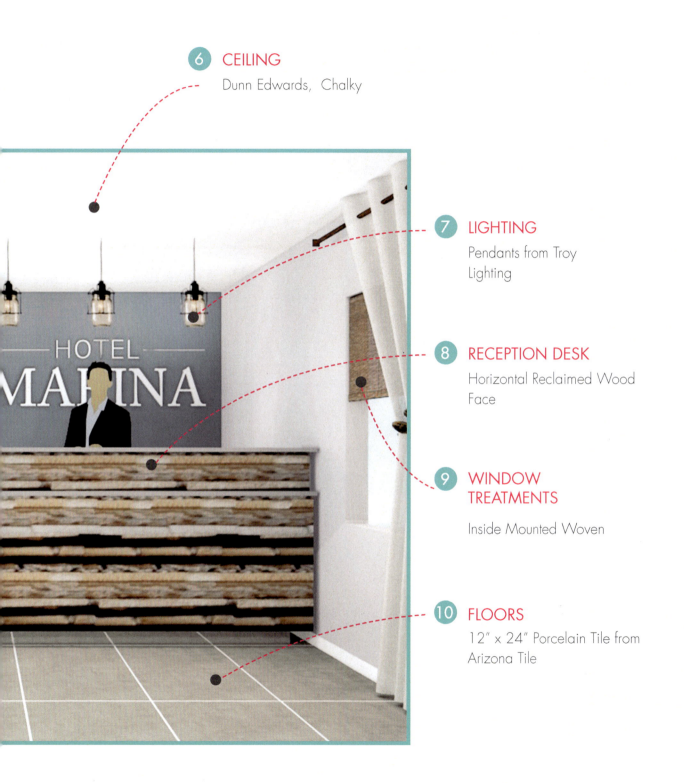

6 CEILING
Dunn Edwards, Chalky

7 LIGHTING
Pendants from Troy Lighting

8 RECEPTION DESK
Horizontal Reclaimed Wood Face

9 WINDOW TREATMENTS
Inside Mounted Woven

10 FLOORS
12" x 24" Porcelain Tile from Arizona Tile

PAINT-BY-NUMBERS DECORATING

BEFORE & AFTERS

Before

Dream Home-In-A-Box

IMAGINE THE POSSIBILITIES

After

PAINT-BY-NUMBERS DECORATING

BEFORE & AFTERS

Before

Dream Home-In-A-Box

IMAGINE THE POSSIBILITIES

After

PAINT-BY-NUMBERS DECORATING

BEFORE & AFTERS

Before

Dream Home-In-A-Box

IMAGINE THE POSSIBILITIES

After

PAINT-BY-NUMBERS DECORATING

BEFORE & AFTERS

Before

Dream Home-In-A-Box

238 INSTANT DREAM HOME

IMAGINE THE POSSIBILITIES

After

PAINT-BY-NUMBERS DECORATING

BEFORE & AFTERS

Before

Dream Home-In-A-Box

IMAGINE THE POSSIBILITIES

After

PAINT-BY-NUMBERS DECORATING

BEFORE & AFTERS

Before

Dream Home-In-A-Box

242 INSTANT DREAM HOME

IMAGINE THE POSSIBILITIES

After

PAINT-BY-NUMBERS DECORATING

BEFORE & AFTERS

Before

Dream Home-In-A-Box

IMAGINE THE POSSIBILITIES

After

PAINT-BY-NUMBERS DECORATING

BEFORE & AFTERS

Before

Dream Home-In-A-Box

IMAGINE THE POSSIBILITIES

After

PAINT-BY-NUMBERS DECORATING

BEFORE & AFTERS

Before

Dream Home-In-A-Box

IMAGINE THE POSSIBILITIES

After

PAINT-BY-NUMBERS DECORATING

BEFORE & AFTERS

Before

Dream Home-In-A-Box

250 INSTANT DREAM HOME

IMAGINE THE POSSIBILITIES

After

IMAGINE THE POSSIBILITIES

GIVE YOURSELF THE GIFT OF A HOME YOU'LL SIMPLY LOVE

If you've made it this far and you still have questions, don't worry. If you're stuck or simply have questions regarding your home then let's talk. I'd be more than happy to help guide you one step closer towards your dream home.

IMAGINE THE POSSIBILITIES

SCHEDULE A 60 MINUTE INTERIOR DESIGN CONSULTATION

BOOK AN APPOINTMENT:

SIMPLYSTUNNINGSPACES.NET
ENTER CODE: INSTANT DREAM HOME

THE BUSINESS OF DESIGN

HOW TO TURN YOUR CREATIVE PASSION INTO A WELL PAYING BUSINESS

THE BUSINESS OF INTERIOR DESIGN

THE BUSINESS OF DESIGN
HOW TO TURN YOUR CREATIVE PASSION INTO A WELL PAYING BUSINESS

"If you're anything like me, you either express yourself through creativity, or you have an entrepreneurial spirit that drives you. Learning how to combine these two is the key to success in this field."

I've had this crazy entrepreneurial spirit ever since I was eleven years old. I used to make and sell hair scrunchies to the girls at school; one for $3 or two for $5. Back in my hometown of Colchester, Vermont I was always working, all through middle school and high school. From paper routes to babysitting, restaurants and grocery stores, I did every job I could find and sometimes two at a time. I bartended my way through college and then sold my art skills to a restaurant owner who hired me to paint murals.

Immediately after graduating from the well-established interior design program at Virginia Tech I thought I knew it all. I decided to jump-start my career by moving to Las Vegas, the fastest growing city in the country. I smelled opportunity and didn't hesitate a bit to uproot myself.

After arriving in Las Vegas, I quickly networked my way in with the movers and shakers of the town. Only a few months later, I landed my first interior design client from a luxury real estate broker I had met. My first business, Darcy K Designs, was born.

This first client, whom to this day is still a good friend of mine, was convinced I could help him with his new home simply based on the glowing referral. Luckily my natural creative knack served me well and I put some of my technical design skills to the test too. However, I quickly realized that I had no idea how to make any real money as a Designer.

I had taken a few business classes in school but none of which seemed to come in handy at the time. On top of that, I didn't have any resources or connections to help me bring my ideas to life. The road to my own successful interior design business suddenly seemed much further away than I had imagined.

I decided it would be best to get a job working for an interior design company. Through another referral I landed a great job with a booming design firm and started designing model homes for real estate developers. It was through this real-world experience that I gained most of my

THE BUSINESS OF INTERIOR DESIGN

knowledge of the business of interior design.

Happy with the job, but not content with the income I was bringing in, I created a second position for myself within the company- Marketing Director. It was here where I taught myself the value of relationships, how to sell interior design services and how to make a good living doing something I truly loved to do.

My entrepreneurial spirit was in full force; I knew the city was booming with high-rise condos and I wanted to make sure we were getting a piece of the action.

Within the first few weeks of taking on this position I eagerly landed the biggest sales presentation this company had ever seen. It was for one of the hottest real estate developers in the city who was building a new high-rise condo tower on the strip. My pitch was for us to put in a small design studio in their building, so we would be the "go-to" designers for anyone in the building. Part of the deal I would make of course meant commission on anything we sold out of that design center.

I continued my eighty-hour work weeks thinking I would be set for years to come if I kept up this pace. My boss was flying me to Paris for design shows, we were chauffeuring limos around the city to showcase our work. Life was fun and exciting and I was confident starting my career in Vegas was the right move.

Until Vegas got slick, right under my feet. I parted ways with this company after they selfishly decided to cut my commissions in half (after the deal had closed). I vowed never to work for anyone else ever again.

My first new business was not a glamorous one but it helped me pay my bills. I didn't have time to waste at this point, I had been living a very cozy life and had accumulated over $4,500 per month in expenses and I had to make ends meet fast. I started a business selling artwork on the side of the road.

My first day selling art was one I'll never forget. I put my ego aside and parked a uhaul filled with art in a parking lot in Summerland. Not two hours in, my art display was perfectly arranged on easels for the busy road travelers to see. Suddenly, the sky turned grey and the wind started howling. For the first and only time, in my five years of living in Vegas, it started to hail. Not just any old hail either, I'm talking golf balls flying from the sky kind of hail. Paintings were flying everywhere. It was like being in the movie the Wizard of Oz. I was chasing paintings left and right and suddenly, before I could catch it, a small rooster painting went flying through the sky and landed on a branch lying on the ground. It ripped a hole right down the middle of the rooster's chest. My

THE BUSINESS OF INTERIOR DESIGN

first day back in the entrepreneurial trenches and I was already at a loss. Life sure was tough back then.

Ten years later, I can honestly say, that I have made just about every mistake in the book at least once. These mistakes cost me money, no doubt. I also spent three years of my time getting a sweat equity MBA in the world of business, internet marketing and coaching. I worked with nationally recognized business coaches, famous real estate gurus, savvy Internet marketers and other Interior Designers.

I spent the past four years building my design business in the city of my dreams- San Diego, California. Business is good here and I get to spend my days helping homeowners and businesses with their design needs. Every project is different, every client is unique and there are new and exciting challenges every day. My creativity is stretched daily and the satisfaction at the end of every project propels me to do even better at the next.

It appears to my colleagues that my business was built almost overnight. Yet I look back on all of the challenges I had and have imagined how much faster it could've been had I known only half of what I know now. This realization is what encouraged me to develop a coaching program for other aspiring Interior Designers and Creative Entrepreneurs.

If you're interested in harnessing your creativity into a successful business you will love and can manage from the comfort of your home then reach out. I'd love to help get you on the right path and steer you away from the detours that will only slow you down.

THE BUSINESS OF INTERIOR DESIGN

WANT TO START OR GROW YOUR OWN INTERIOR DESIGN BUSINESS?

VISIT: **SIMPLYSTUNNINGPSACES.NET/INTERIORDESIGNSCHOOL**

STAY IN TOUCH

Here's all the ways in which you and I can get to know each other just a little bit better:

1. Get some face-to-face time with me as I walk you through the basics of this book at: instantdreamhome.com

2. Find more inspiring pictures & projects: simplystunningspaces.net/gallery

3. Get the latest news & special offers by "liking" our facebook fan page: facebook.com/simplystunningspaces

4. Read (or write.) glowing reviews at: yelp.com/biz/simply-stunning-spaces-san-diego

5. Get a sneak peak into the behind the scenes of homes of celebrity clients at: simplystunningspaces.net/videos

6. Watch my collection of How-to Videos: www.Designtube.tv

7. Check out the TV pilot we filmed with Kiptyn Locke at: female-eye.com

8. Watch our interview with Bruce Buffer at: celebritybachelorpads.com

9. Book a consultation: simplystunningspaces.net. Click on "BOOK APPOINTMENT".

10. Apply for my Interior Designer Coaching Program: simplystunningspaces.net/interiordesignschool

I'd love to hear from you and hope you'll get connected with me one way or another.

ACKNOWLEDGEMENTS

This book wouldn't be complete without mentioning the people in my life who have been there with me since the very beginning, encouraging me through every stage of building this business. To my parents, Cliff and Ruthann Kempton who have always encouraged me to follow my dreams and supported me in every way they possibly could. For never questioning my crazy ideas, never steering me away from my entrepreneurial spirit and always giving me the love and support I needed to keep my head held high. For providing a foundation of faith that I could hang my hat on when times got rough, I can't thank you enough.

To the love of my life and biggest fan, Ryan you are everything and more than I could've ever hoped for. I feel so blessed every day knowing that I have you by my side, pushing me to be my very best. Your love, support and encouragement mean the world to me.

To each one of my clients for opening up their homes and hearts to me. And to all of my savvy business-minded friends & mentors for sharing your expertise and advice. To my right-hand woman, Diana Thai for all the years of dedication and heart you put into everything you do.

And to everyone else who's love, support and friendship has impacted my life year after year: Tom & Judy Shailor, Sarah-Ki, Phil, Connie, Erika, Kristi, Lindsey Jean, George, Marzena, Mia, Xenia, Stephen Boykin, David Phan, Jason Stroder, Dennis, Chris Lenahan, and all the rest of you, thank you.

Made in the USA
San Bernardino, CA
19 February 2017